DEDICATION

To families and friends who gather
to celebrate the beauty of winter.

AROUNNA
KHOUNNORAJ

Winter Celebrations

A MODERN GUIDE TO A HANDMADE CHRISTMAS

photography by Laura Edwards

Hardie Grant

QUADRILLE

Contents

INTRODUCTION

Opening a bricks and mortar storefront was always one of our goals. A place to work and sell our wares but also a place where customers could visit, see how we worked and connect with the things we make. We found a perfect spot in Toronto, just to the west of downtown, near some parks and a collection of like-minded shops, artists and makers.

Being part of a craft community was about connecting with other artists. It was also about supporting each other through work, collaboration and conversation. And in many ways our shop was a place that we could share with creative friends, so before too long we had a full roster of exhibitions, workshops and markets throughout the year. My favourite was our annual holiday market every December. Joined by family and fellow artists we would all decorate the space and fill the front window with handmade items and ornaments specially made for the event.

But our shop wasn't just for work – it was also our home and before too long we were working alongside a couple of little ones taking part in all the holiday activities. As a family of makers we've always encouraged creativity, and having everyone involved makes it a meaningful experience for everybody. When they are young, it's not unusual for kids to see that gift giving is also about making. I always looked forward to getting poorly wrapped presents with crumpled wrapping paper decorated with drawings and writing. Those are the things that make holidays even more memorable. And whenever possible I still believe that handmade gifts are the best – they are personal, making them unique and special.

In the years since our work has expanded in so many ways, with travel and teaching, developing craft projects for social media, and three project books already in print. But our holiday traditions, in our shop and at home, are still my favourite times. So, it made perfect sense to put together a collection of projects that celebrate the holiday season as a time of making. Projects that find inventive ways to decorate, wrap and make gifts using a range of techniques suitable for any skill level. Projects that reflect our design ethos of being creative with everyday materials, including many things you may already have on hand, in ways that are simple and modern.

My hope is that this book will inspire readers and suggest new possibilities for making with friends and family.

HOW TO USE THIS BOOK

Making decorations and gifts for the holidays allows you to express yourself in ways that store bought items cannot. There is just something about handmade items; the materials and qualities mean anything you make will be uniquely 'you'. And one of the joys of making is sharing that experience with others. I've always loved making ornaments and wrapping paper with our kids, and creating handmade gifts will make anyone feel special. With that in mind, my intention with this book was to collect a wide range of projects that we have made over the years – items from our studio work as well as our own holiday traditions – and combine them with techniques and materials that have always been important to my work. I've placed an emphasis on materials that are readily available and reflect the natural qualities that I love, with various techniques that don't require a lot of tools or equipment and are accessible for anyone with any skill level. And these are projects that can be worked on over a period of time, so that you can pick them up whenever you have a moment.

I've organized the book into two main sections – Decoration and Gift – both containing a range of projects using various materials and techniques, but each with a different focus. In Decorations, I've gathered projects to create seasonal settings throughout your home. Items to hang as tree ornaments or to accentuate walls and window settings, and with a special focus on ideas to decorate your table with centrepieces, overhead garlands and to personalize individual place settings. In Gift, I've included a wide range of handmade gifts that are as imaginative as they are useful. Things that won't take too long to make and can easily be customized. You can add your own expressive elements or – even better – you can personalize them with specific recipients in mind. There are enough projects to cover anyone on your list, and they will hopefully encourage everyone to bring back the tradition of making gifts. In addition, to complete your gift-giving needs, I've included creative ways to make your own wrapping.

Each project contains all the information you will need along with step-by-step instructions, drawings and photographs. We'll have discussions on all relevant techniques and suggested materials used, and I'll provide some hints to further personalize your work. You will find that some projects are quite simple, while others are more complex with additional steps that sometimes involve multiple techniques. With that in mind, I think you will find that there will be plenty to occupy anyone who wishes to closely follow my steps. But how precisely you follow my steps is entirely up to you. In one sense, the instructions are just guidelines that will allow you to achieve your desired results. But in reality, creativity is full of variables. My approach is quite often intuitive; gathering information but modifying certain things when

I need to, and adding elements or changing the look of something to suit my particular vision. So, if you like, feel free to adjust projects to meet your experience as a maker and allow yourself to express your own ideas as well. If you should want a bigger challenge, projects can easily be modified by adding additional elements or details. This is important for the things we make – they are always better with our own personal touch, especially when they are a gift or will be adorning our home. So, once you feel confident, think of these projects as inspiration as much as instruction. In this way, everything you make will be your own, and you'll always have reason to come back and make new items every time.

One last thought: I have often found that making is not just about expression or creativity, but also about working economically and responsibly. I firmly believe that whenever possible we should use what we have on hand – materials, tools and sometimes even techniques. I always keep my remnants and try not to waste anything, including used or found objects. I find that working this way always results in interesting new combinations and unforeseen surprises.

STITCH LIBRARY

BLIND STITCH

This stitch is used to close openings because the tiny stitches are almost invisible on the right side of the fabric.

Thread your needle and make a quilter's knot at the end (see page 15). Bring the needle up through one folded edge so the knot will be hidden inside. Take a tiny stitch though the opposite layer of fabric, so it will be invisible on the right side, then take a longer stitch through the folded edge.

Continue in this way along the open edge until you have closed the gap, then fasten off.

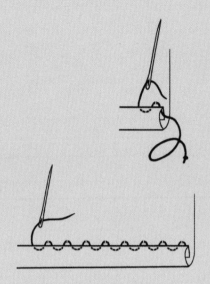

SPLIT STITCH

The split stitch is a basic embroidery stitch that can be used to outline an image or as a filler. It is very similar to a back stitch, but rather than going back to the end of the previous stitch from the top, you stab the previous stitch from below to create a continuous line. To use split stitch as a filler stitch, create an outline of the image then fill in with rows of stitches either next to each other or spaced slightly apart.

First determine your stitch length. Start by bringing the needle up from the back to the front and make a first stitch.

Now, with the needle underneath again, bring your needle up at a spot near the end, but within the previous stitch, thus splitting the threads of the previous stitch. Then make your next stitch.

Repeat to make a line of stitches.

COUCHING

This technique uses two threads, one that is laid down on the surface and one that is stitched over it to hold it in place. You can use two different colour threads, or two the same colour.

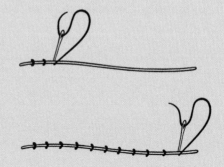

Bring the first thread up through the fabric and lay it along the surface in whatever shape or line you wish. Thread a second needle and bring it up through the fabric just below the line of the laid thread, wrap around it with a tiny vertical whip stitch (see page 16) over the top and go back down into the base cloth near to where you came out. In essence, you are creating a stitch perpendicular to the laid thread to hold it in place. After this first stitch, move along a little and repeat.

Continue along the laid thread until it is held firm with stitches along its entire length. To finish the line, take the laid thread and, underneath, turn it around to run back on top of itself for a length equal to a few stitches. Continue making small whip stitches in the second thread to fasten the folded end to the base cloth. Tie the second thread from below to end the line of stitches.

TOP STITCHING

Top stitching is a visible stitch that is used to finish an edge of an object such as the opening of a bag or pocket. It's a stitch that is not about construction but rather about strengthening an edge or giving it a strong visual presence. This can be done by hand using a backstitch or with a sewing machine.

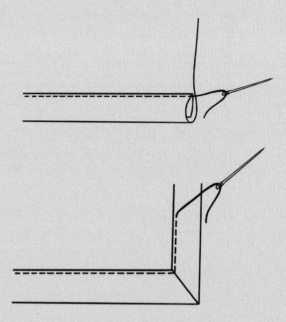

LONG SEED STITCH

A seed stitch consists of simple little stitches used to fill an area.

Sometimes seed stitches appear as a variation of running stitches (see page 16), sharing a common direction but as smaller decorative stitches on top of the fabric. Other times they fill an area more randomly, similar in size, but pointing in any direction so as to appear organic. To create the seed stitch, bring your needle up from below and create a short stitch anywhere on the cloth and then take your needle back down again. Repeat this, with each stitch placed as you see fit – either as a pattern or in slightly different directions without an overall pattern.

Try to keep each stitch similar in length, and more or less equally spaced, scattered over the base cloth. As a variation, you can work the stitches in clusters, with larger spaces between each cluster. To create a long seed stitch, you just need to lengthen your stitches.

STRAIGHT STITCH

A straight stitch is similar to a single running stitch (see page 16) but tends to be considerably longer, creating a line that extends between a start and stop point. This creates a simple linear element of any length that can be used in a number of decorative ways, such as filler stitches, border stitches or as lines within a pictorial motif.

To make a straight stitch bring your needle up from below at the first point, extent the thread across the surface of the fabric and then take the needle back down again at the second point. Either fasten off for a single line, or repeat according to your design.

QUILTER'S KNOT

This knot is used for quilting because you can adjust the size of the knot and it can be hidden between the layers. If you make a small one you can pull through one layer of fabric so it's hidden inbetween. You will need to create a knot before you starting any kind of hand sewing or top stitching. Always cut thread an arm's length and no longer, or it may tangle as you work.

Place the tail on the top edge of the needle and with the other hand pinch the tip. Wrap the thread around the needle several times – how many times determines how big the knot will be.

Pinch the wrapped thread with the same finger and push it towards the eye of the needle. As you get to the eye, gently begin to release a bit of your grip.

Pull the wraps down until you reach the bottom of the thread, so that you are pulling the knot and needle away from each other in opposite directions. You'll end up with a neat knot at the end of the thread.

FINISHING KNOT

This is used at the end of a length of hand sewing on the underside of the fabric.

Turn your work over so you are working on the back of the fabric, with the needle and thread on this side. Take your needle under the last stitch on this side and pull the thread until a loop forms.

Pass the needle through the loop. Pull until a knot is formed.

To secure the knot further you can repeat the steps for a larger knotif you prefer. Clip the thread end to 5 mm (¼ in).

RUNNING STITCH

A running stitch is one of the most common stitches used in all types of hand sewing. In appearance it resembles a continuous line of little dashes. I usually try to keep the distance between stitches equal to the length of the actual stitches, but you may modify any spacing for visual impact. Loading the needle allows you to work faster than working one stitch at a time.

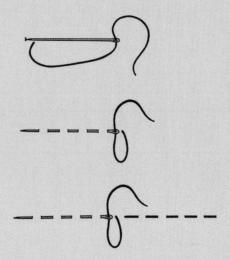

Pull the needle through the fabric from underneath until the knot hits the fabric. Next, 'load' the stitches onto your needle, about three at a time depending on the length of the needle, in an under-and-overmethod, then pull the needle and thread through to get the resulting dashes. Repeat as many times as necessary.

WHIP STITCH

A whip stitch is similar to a running stitch (above) in that it is a continuous line of stitches with visible spaces inbetween. But rather than appearing as a series of dashes in a single direction, they are stitched either on an angle or even perpendicular to the direction of the stitch line. Whip stitches can be used anywhere but are more commonly used along the edges where layers of fabric are sewn together, where two pieces of fabric are joined together, or where smaller pieces of fabric are sewn onto larger pieces.

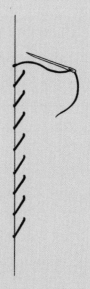

Start your whip stitch underneath and bring the needle up through the fabric you wish to join. Make a stitch over the edge at the angle of your choice. Now, go underneath again to a position next to the previous stitch, then up through the fabric and over the edge.

Repeat until the edges of the fabric are sewn together. The edges of the fabric can be rolled under to form a neat edge or left raw.

TACKING (BASTING) STITCH

When the stitches and spacing of running stitch becomes much longer (about 2.5 cm/1 in) then it is considered to be a tacking stitch, which is commonly used to temporarily hold together layers of fabric prior to permanent stitches. It can be used as a replacement for pins and is usually cut away after the final sewing is finished.

Follow the instructions for a running stitch (opposite) but load your needle with fewer, longer stitches, and keep them rather loose so that they are easy to snip and remove.

APPLIQUÉ STITCH

Appliqué is a technique where fabric shapes are sewn onto large pieces of cloth in order to decorate a surface. It is thought of as an ornamental form of needlework where fabric pieces are used to create pictures, patterns and compositions, or representational images. A variety of stitches such as blind and whip stitches (see page 12 and opposite) can be used along the edges of the fabric to attach the layers.

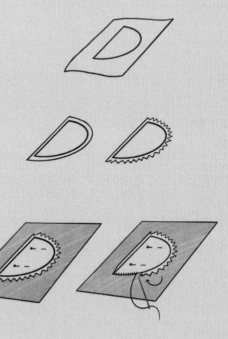

Both appliqué and patching often use the same set of stitches, but the intent and effect of appliqué is significantly different. Patching typically uses single fabric pieces that are geometric or organic, while appliqué is an ornamental form of needlework where fabric pieces are used to create pictures, patterns and compositions, or representational images. Stitches can be used along the edges of the fabric to attach the layers. For a finished look tuck the edges under as you stitch, or leave a raw edge for a softer look that emphasizes the nature of the material.

Decoration

Place Settings

When it comes to place settings I prefer designs that are a little understated; they may have charm and perhaps some whimsey, but they can work with the other elements of my table. For these place settings I chose a simple belly band wrapping for napkins with cut images of flowers, which just happens to be my favourite decorative theme. They are really simple to make with just the minimum of materials and can be easily personalized with the names of each guest.

YOU WILL NEED

Templates on page 158

Masking tape

Pencil

15 x 28 cm (6 x 11 in) light-to medium-weight
   paper for each place setting

Fine craft knife with a small blade

Cutting mat

TIPS

— I used Canson Ingres paper, which is 105 gsm (27 lb) – slightly heavier that standard bond – in a cream colour, but feel free to use any colour that suits your table setting.
— The size of paper I chose meant that when my napkin was folded the long side of the paper could completely wrap around the napkin while the short side would allow a little bit of napkin to be seen above and below. You can adjust the paper sizing to suit your napkin.
— If your napkin bundle is larger than your paper band you can punch a hole on either side of the edge at the back, thread a short piece of string or ribbon through and tie a knot.

Copy the template of the design you wish to use and tape it onto a light source, such as a window. Place your paper on top so that the image is centred left to right and top to bottom and secure with masking tape. If you plan to write the name of the guest onto each place setting, then leave a little extra space below the image. Lightly trace each image onto your paper using a pencil.

Next, place the paper on a cutting mat and cut along the lines with your craft knife. Keep in mind that in some areas you will only be cutting lines and in other areas you will be cutting out areas completely. Please use the template as a reference to which elements to keep and which to cut away. Try to cut without the aid of a ruler so that your image has a hand drawn quality.

Once you have cut all the areas, use your fingers or the tip of the knife to fold the paper up from the back so that the flaps sit up and you can see through the paper. This gives the images a textural and three-dimensional quality. As an option you can place a different colour paper underneath, but I chose to leave it open so that colour of the napkin would be part of the image.

Wrap the belly band around the folded napkin, joining the 2 sides with a piece of tape on the back, and place in the centre of each plate.

Ornaments

Ornaments can come in any form, made from many materials with different techniques, but hanging them together in eclectic mixes is so much fun. Textile ornaments are particularly close to my heart, and can easily be made in an array of wintertime figures. These ones are each adorned with embroidered details that speak of the hand-made, so you will want to use them year after year. Along with these I've also made paper snowflakes that really capture the translucent quality of ice, and will glow from surrounding lights. They are made from materials that are easily sourced, and you might just already have around your home.

EMBROIDERED ORNAMENTS

These embroidered ornaments are stuffed with wool roving and made with a combination of coloured fabric and stitches. Textile objects always have a lovely texture and feel and are perfect to decorate with, or make a set to give as a gift.

YOU WILL NEED

Templates on the back endpaper

Low tack tape

25 cm (¼ yd) of cotton quilting weight
 fabric (in a variety of colours)

Water-soluble fabric marker

Embroider hoop (optional)

Stranded cotton embroidery
 thread (floss)

No. 3 embroidery needle

Snips and scissors

Water spritzer

1.8 m (2 yd) of cotton string for
 hanging ornaments

Sewing machine and matching thread

Wool roving or fibrefill for stuffing

Chopstick or small stick

— Note that the leaf ornament was sewn together and stuffed first before it was embroidered so that it has a puffy look. Work steps 3 to 5 first, then embroider.

Copy one of the templates and then tape it onto a light source, and place the fabric on top. Trace the template with the water-soluble marker onto your fabric. You can also draw the design freehand. Remember to leave some fabric around the shape to add the seam allowance later.

(1) Once you've traced the design, embroider inside the shape by either using a hoop or holding the fabric in your hand. To use a hoop, place the inner hoop underneath the fabric and the outer ring on top with the fabric in between. Tighten the hoop while pulling the fabric down all around until it is taut.

Embroidery stitches used:
Tree: long seed stitch (2 strands of thread)
Bird: split stitch (6 strands of thread)
Round: split stitch (6 strands of thread)
Star: straight stitch (3 strands of thread)
Leaf: back stitch (3 strands of thread).

Once you finished embroidering the pattern, spritz the surface with a little water to make any visible drawn lines disappear and wait until it dries before sewing. Then, cut around your shape making sure to add a 1 cm (⅜ in) seam allowance all around. Cut a second piece the same size for the back.

(2) Place the back on top of the front with right sides together. At the top of the ornament place a loop of cotton string in between the layers with the loop side on the inside and the ends extending out by about 2.5 cm (1 in). Cut the string however long you want it to be; I keep mine 38 cm (15 in) long.

(3) Sew around the edge with a 1 cm (⅜ in) seam allowance, leaving an opening around 5 cm (2 in) on one side to turn right side out. Before you do this make sure to snip the seam allowance along any curves to avoid any puckering in those areas.

Turn right sides out and stuff with wool roving or fibrefill. Use a small stick, such as a chopstick, to push out and fill the small areas with stuffing. Use a blind stitch (see page 12) to close the opening. Repeat these steps for all the designs.

PAPER ORNAMENTS

Paper is the perfect material to make ornaments because there are so many different variations using only cutting and folding, and so many different papers that you can use. For this design I used tracing paper and created two sizes: small and large. My favourite thing about using tracing paper is how it captures the light to give the ornaments a glow.

YOU WILL NEED

90 gsm (25 lb) weight tracing paper

Scissors

Pencil

Ruler

Paper glue stick

Hot glue gun

25 cm (10 in) of light weight (115 g / ¼ lb) fishing line for each ornament

Cut the tracing paper into 4 x 9-cm (3½-in) squares for each small ornament, and into 3 x 12.5-cm (5-in) squares for each large ornament. Fold each square into quarters by folding it in half one way and then in half the other way until you have a small square. Draw a series of skinny triangles, a little less than 2.5 cm (1 in) in length, all along one of the open sides. Make sure you are not drawing on one of the folded edges. Cut out the triangles with your scissors and when you open it up you will have 2 straight sides and 2 sides with triangles cut out.

Create an accordion fold along the straight side with each fold about 0.5 cm (¼ in) deep. Make sure to crease the paper with your nail as you fold to give it a good structure. When you have finished the accordion folding, take each folded piece and fold it lengthwise in half. Using a glue stick, apply glue along the edges where the 2 sides meet and press firmly to hold; you will end up with a triangular shape. Repeat for all the pieces you need for each ornament.

Next glue all the pieces for an ornament together along their edges using a hot glue gun to create a circular shape. As you glue the 2 pieces together add a loop of fishing line so that the ends are attached within a glue line.

TIPS

— As an option, if you want the ornament to have more density you can glue the smaller size on top of the larger size. Also, keep in mind this method can be used with any paper – it would be fun to experiment with other types such as wrapping paper or coloured stock.

Paper Garland

A garland is a lovely way to decorate a doorway, mantle, ceiling or wall. And every time you put it up it will always seem new, taking on new shapes and patterns as it hangs in different ways. I especially like this one because of its botanical reference – it reminds me of a little bit of ivy. I decided to use wire instead of string because I like that you can bend and manipulate how the piece hangs and moves. The leaves on this garland are all the same but have a nice organic feel due to the twisting of the wire support, and they are really easy to make with simple repeated folds. You can make them colourful with different papers if you like, although I prefer quiet tones that always work well with the other decorations in the room.

YOU WILL NEED

Template on page 156–157

Pencil

Thin cardboard, such as a cereal box

Paper scissors

25 x 25 cm (10 x 10 in) of kraft paper for each leaf

38 cm (15 in) of 24 gauge copper wire for each leaf

Wire cutters

Paper glue stick

Nails and hammer for hanging

— I used kraft paper to make the leaf shapes on the garland. When you cut paper for folding make sure that you know which direction the grain of the paper is going – you will find that it is much easier to fold paper with the grain. If the paper bends easily and you don't feel resistance, that means your folds are going with the grain. This will determine the direction you should place your template.

— You can also use wrapping paper or wallpaper to create this project.

(1) Copy the leaf template to create a cardboard pattern 12.5 x 24 cm (5 x 9½ in), and then cut out the shape. Fold each square of kraft paper in half going against the grain and place the pattern on top of the paper with the straight long side against the fold of the paper. Using a pencil, trace around the pattern and cut with scissors along your drawn line. Open the folded paper and lay flat.

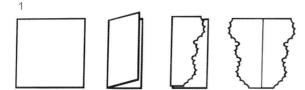

(2) Make a series of accordion folds across the entire leaf shape using a 1.25 cm (½ in) crease. Make the folds with the grain of the paper and perpendicular to the initial fold from step 1. Start with the large end and continue the accordion fold until you get to the small end.

(3) Bend each 38 cm (15 in) length of wire in half loosely. At the midway point, where the wire is bending, shape the bend so it is squarish with an end about 1.25 cm (½ in) deep.

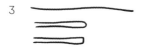

(4) When you finish all the accordion folds in each leaf, hold the leaf shape with all the folds closed tight. Place the flat end of the wire at the midway point, with the ends of the wire extending out from the side with the short folds. Then twist the wire ends until you have a twist about 4 cm (1½ in) long, and all the folds are held tightly closed.

(5) Fold the entire length of a leaf in half, on the opposite side to the wire ends, so that the long sides of the folds are now facing each other. Attach these 2 sides together with a glue stick and firmly press the glued sides together. Once the glue dries you can gently pull out the folds to create a fan shape. Repeat this process to create as many leaves as you want. For the garland in the photo on page 31, I made 19 leaves but you make as many as you want for your length of garland.

Bend the wire ends on each leaf in opposite directions so that the 2 ends resemble an upside-down letter T. Then connect the leaves to each other by twisting the wire end of one leaf with the wire of another leaf. When all are joined, the entire garland can be hung on nails in any arrangement you like.

Wreath

I've always loved brass; its shine and warm colour combined with a softness that makes it so easy to work with. So it's perfect for creating botanical designs, such as wreaths with all the shapes and details, which will last for many years as part of your holiday decor. This project may appear challenging, but it is a very straightforward design that lets all the imperfections of bent wire and metal become part of its charm. However if you'd rather you can use a shiny, coloured or plain paper instead of the brass.

YOU WILL NEED

Template on page 155

Thin cardboard, such as a cereal box

Pencil

Scissors

Gloves

5 brass sheets, 0.127 mm (0.005 in) thick, each 10 x 25 cm (4 x 10 in)

Ballpoint pen

Kitchen shears

Fine sandpaper (optional)

Marking tool with a dull point, such as a knitting needle

Scrap wood

Hammer

Nail similar in thickness to the 22 gauge wire

7.5 m (8 yd) of brass wire, 22 gauge

Wire cutters

Needle nose pliers

91.5 cm (36 in) of slightly heavier brass wire, about 14 gauge

25 cm (10 in) of leather cord

TIPS

— Five sheets of brass, sized at 10 x 25 cm (4 x 10 in), will make about 55 leaves.
— The metal is thin enough that you could also use an old pair of regular scissors to cut it if that's what you have on hand.

Copy the leaf template onto cardboard and cut out. Place the cardboard cutout on one of the brass sheets and outline the shape using a ballpoint pen. Trace as many leaf shapes as possible from each sheet. Try to lay out your shapes in a strategic manner so as to not have a lot of waste. I usually line them up in rows so that each row is tucked into the negative space of the previous row. You will need about 55 leaves.

Use your shears or old scissors to cut out the shapes. Please take care while cutting metal and wear gloves because the edges will be a bit sharp. As an option you can lightly sand the edges with a fine sandpaper to make the edges less sharp. Once all the leaves are cut out, draw on the veins using the dull point of the knitting needle. By pressing firmly as you draw you will cause the leaves to bend slightly. This will give them a nice organic quality.

(1) Place a metal leaf good side facing up on top of the flat scrap of wood, then place the nail about 0.5 cm (¼ in) from the bottom point. Hammer the nail gently to make a small hole just big enough for the thin wire to go through. If any small burrs on the edge of the hole result you can gently tap these flat with your hammer, while making sure the hole remains open. Repeat for all the leaves.

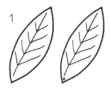

Cut the 7.5 m (8 yd) of wire into 3 equal sections. If you find that length of wire is too long for you to work with, cut it shorter. Slide a leaf onto the wire through the hole.

(2) At the midpoint of one section of wire create a little 'U' shaped bend, about 0.5 cm (¼ in) deep, using your needle nose pliers. Slide the leaf down the wire and into the little bend that you created. Then pinch the little bend in the wire and twist twice so that the leaf is locked in position. Leave the leaf to point in whichever direction it wants – this will give it a nice organic sense of movement.

Continue to attach leaves in both directions along the wire, leaving a varying distance of about 5–10 cm (2–4 in) between each leaf, and leaving about 15 cm (6 in) of wire free at each end. Repeat on each section of wire until you have 3 strands of leaves.

Bend small circular hooks on each end of the heavier gauge brass wire using your pliers. Then bend the wire into a loose circle and hook the ends together to create a circular structure around which you will wrap the strands of leaves. You can forgo this step if you want your wreath to hang loosely with less structure. Work flat on a table and be mindful that the leaves can be sharp – again use gloves if you like. Start by wrapping one end of the wire around the hoop a few times and then loosely running the strands around the hoop, only occasionally wrapping them through and around the hoop. At the end, wrap the end of the strands in the same manner as at the start. Repeat with the other strands, keeping each strand loose and not too structured. Let the leaves arrange themselves randomly. Add a hanging string at the top – I used a small leather cord.

Tablecloth

Meals during holiday times are important – the food, the table, the settings and, of course, family and friends. Having a custom tablecloth to gather around really sets the mood for the whole event. But there is no reason that holidays should have a monopoly on a nicely set table. So, for this tablecloth, I wanted a design that would not only be great for holidays but would make any meal special. While this project may seem large, I've made the stitching simple by using a running stitch with a smaller space between stitches. By doing so the stitching seems continuous with a denser line, allowing the shapes to appear stronger. Even so, the natural colours and repeated botanical shape have a subtlety that will easily work with the rest of your decor.

YOU WILL NEED

Tablecloth, any weight will work

Sewing machine (optional)

Hand sewing needle and thread (optional)

Template on page 156–157

Paper

Pencil

Thin cardboard, such as a cereal box

Snips and scissors

Water-soluble fabric marker

Indigo sashiko thread, no. 5 perle cotton thread, or stranded cotton embroidery thread (floss)

Embroidery needle with large enough eye for the thread

Thimble

TIPS

— This project can be created with a preowned or a ready-made tablecloth. For mine, I used a length of hemp canvas fabric cut to fit my table. If you are making your own, make sure that the fabric is large enough so that it hangs over the table edges by at least 30 cm (12 in) all around.

— I used indigo thread for my stitching, but any contrasting colour will work.

(1) If you are making your own tablecloth, start by sewing a rolled hem all around the edge. Starting at a corner, fold a few inches of the fabric edge over twice to the wrong side, by about 0.5 cm (¼ in) each time, and smooth with your fingers. Stitch by hand or with your sewing machine from the corner, sewing close to the edge of the inside fold with a coordinating thread colour. Stitch as far you have folded the fabric, then stop, fold another length, and then sew. Repeat this until all 4 edges are complete. Once you finish stitching, press the edges with an iron. Alternatively, fold a hem along all edges, ironing flat as you go, and then sew along the flattened hem.

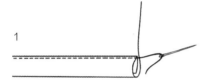

Copy the template to size, or hand draw the shape onto paper to size. Cut out the shape and use it to trace the motif onto the piece of thin cardboard, then cut out. Trace around the shape onto the tablecloth using the water-soluble fabric marker – you can also use a pencil, just keep in mind some lines might show if you draw them too thick. Start by placing a motif in a corner and work outwards, scattering motifs all around the tablecloth in a random manner. Try not to repeat the same placement of motifs next to each other – try to rotate or shift the positions of the shapes as you draw. I separated each motif by a minimum of about 10 cm (4 in). This gives a nice balance of shape and space. Remember that the closer the shapes are to each other, the more you must stitch. Also, try to place the shapes evenly and avoid large or uneven gaps. It's fine if you have to crop a shape along the edge.

Thread your needle with an arm's length of the indigo thread – if using stranded cotton, use all 6 strands. If your fabric is densely woven, try using a shorter length of thread to avoid wear or breakages (you won't encounter this issue if your fabric is more loosely woven). Tie a quilter's knot (see page 15) on the end of your thread and, starting on the wrong side, bring your needle up to the top and all the way out. (2) Using a running stitch (see page 16) follow your drawn lines, loading your needle with stitches about 0.5 cm (¼ in) long with a smaller spaces of about 0.25cm (⅛ in) or less in between. Be aware of your tension while stitching and don't pull on the thread to avoid any puckering. Make sure to flatten the stitching out as you proceed and tie off your threads with knots underneath when necessary. Continue until all of the shapes are stitched. When the piece is finished you just need to give it a press with an iron.

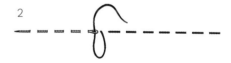

Advent Calendars

An advent calendar is a lovely way to build up holiday excitement. Every day has a little treat or a small gift to share with your family. And gifts can consist of anything really – small things you might make, ornaments to decorate the Christmas tree, and of course sweet treats. But don't stop there – how about a line in a story that every day builds to an exciting finale, or a piece of a picture that is a mystery until the end? Advent calendars come in so many variations, but here are two versions.

FABRIC ADVENT CALENDAR

This reusable fabric calendar for each and every year has an array of pockets and embroidered numbers, perfect for those who don't mind the extra time it takes to sew.

YOU WILL NEED

56 x 81.25 cm (22 x 32 in) of linen fabric for body front

56 x 81.25 cm (22 x 32 in) of backing fabric (calico/cotton muslin or light weight canvas for more structure)

Sewing machine and thread to match linen fabric

Hand sewing needle

Iron

75 x 112 cm (30 x 44 in) of linen fabric for pockets

Ruler or tape measure

Snips and scissors

Water-soluble fabric marker

2.75 m (3 yd) of cream coloured aran (worsted) yarn

2 skeins of red cotton embroidery (floss) thread

No. 3 embroidery needle

Pins

White glue (optional)

(1) Place the 56 x 81.25 cm (22 x 32 in) pieces of linen and backing fabric right sides together with all sides aligned. With your sewing machine, sew along all 4 sides with a 1 cm (⅜ in) seam allowance, leaving an opening about 10 cm (4 in) wide in one side. Pull right sides out through the unsewn opening, then hand sew the opening closed using a blind stitch (see page 12). Top stitch (see page 13) around the entire edge of the piece. Press the fabric with an iron and set aside.

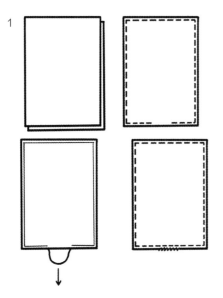

(2) Cut the 75 x 112 cm (30 x 44 in) linen fabric into 5 strips each measuring 15 x 112 cm (6 x 44 in). On each strip sew a 0.5 cm (¼ in) rolled hem along one long side and press with an iron (this will be the top of the pockets). Fold the other long side under by 0.5 cm (¼ in) and press with an iron, but leave unsewn.

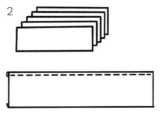

(3) Next, fold and iron each of the fabric strips to create a series of accordion folds that make the rows of pockets. To start, lay one strip on your ironing board, right side facing up, with the rolled hem along the top. On the left end, fold and press the fabric under to the wrong side by 0.5 cm (¼ in) to create a hem along the side. Next, fold the fabric with right sides together and press to create an accordion fold 2.5 cm (1 in) deep, facing to the left and with the fold aligned with the hem edge. Then, 10 cm (4 in) to the right of this fold, create and iron a second accordion fold, also 2.5 cm (1 in) deep, but this time facing to the right. You have just finished one pocket. Now repeat with a 2.5 cm (1 in) deep accordion fold facing left and, 10 cm (4 in) to the right, another 2.5 cm (1 in) deep accordion fold facing right to make 5 pockets along the strip. End the strip on the right-hand side, in the same manner as you started, with a 0.5 cm (¼ in) fold for a hem along the edge. Trim off any extra fabric.

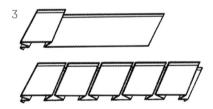

3

Once all the fabric strips have been folded and ironed, draw the numbers freehand from 1 to 25 with a water-soluble marker, centred on each pocket. I made the numbers 6.5 cm (2½ in) high, starting 3 cm (1¼ in) down from the top of the hem. There will be more space under each number as we have yet to make a hem along the bottom edge.

(4) Lay down the cream yarn onto the surface of a pocket along the drawn number. To hold down the yarn, use a couching stitch (see page 13) in a contrasting colour (I used red). Thread the embroidery needle with a length of embroidery cotton and knot the end. Start by coming up from the wrong side at one end of a yarn number and work perpendicular couching stitches slightly less than 0.5 cm (¼ in) apart over the length of cream yarn until the entire number is stitched, finishing with a knot underneath. Repeat for all the numbers.

4

(5) Now sew the pockets to the body of the advent calendar. Start at the bottom (numbers 21–25), by placing this strip 2.5 cm (1 in) up from the bottom the edge,

aligning the pocket edges with the body on the left and right. Pin the piece down so that all the folds are neat and even. First, stitch the 0.5 cm (¼ in) folds at the left and right sides to the edge of the calendar body. Next sew a double line of stitches along the entire bottom of the pockets, through all the folded layers, making sure that the folds stay in place. Stitch the first line close to edge of the hem, and another about 0.5 cm (¼ in) above. Lastly, sew a vertical line of stitches within the fold at the mid points between each pocket. Repeat this step for all the remaining strips of pockets, making sure that the strips are 2.5 cm (1 in) apart.

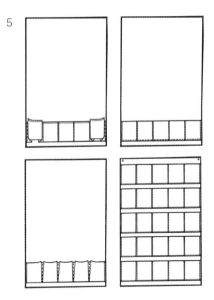

5

To hang the advent calendar you can simply use pins on the corners or you can add a grommet to each corner instead and hang with string or hooks. If you like you can also sew fabric loops across the top to take a wood dowel for hanging.

CLAY NUMBERS ADVENT CALENDAR

This second version uses numbered tags made from clay that can be attached to small paper bags or pouches, which can then be strung together in a variety of ways.

YOU WILL NEED

25 small advent gifts

25 small paper bags

Hole punch

3 lengths of heavy twine, each long enough to hang 8 or 9 bags

Nails and hammer for hanging

5.5 m (6 yd) of baker's string or similar

Ruler or tape measure

Scissors

Set of 25 clay numbers, or you could use wooden or cardboard numbers

Place a small gift inside each paper bag and fold the top of the bag down with a 5 cm (2 in) flap (the flap dimension could change depending on the size of the item you are placing inside). In the middle of the flap, punch 2 holes with a 2.5 cm (1 in) gap between each hole.

Fix the 3 lengths of twine onto a wall, using a hammer and nails, leaving about 30 cm (12 in) between each row.

Cut the baker's string into 25 lengths, each about 20 cm (8 in) long. Thread a clay number onto one of the lengths then thread the ends through the holes in the bag and tie to one of the hanging lengths of twine with a slip knot that can be untied as each bag is opened.

Repeat to hang all the bags onto the lengths of twine.

TIPS

— I got my clay numbers from Paperboatpress. You can make your own using polymer with the numbers pressed out and rubbed with red paint after baking.
— You can use push pins to hang your bags if the objects inside are not heavy.

Swag and Wall Hangings

Some kinds of decoration are common elements at festivities – both public and private – and when you see them you know there is a celebration going on. Folded paper objects suspended in clusters like snowflakes, or swags – wall hangings, traditionally made of fabric or greenery, hung in a curve between two points – are popular. But as common as these might be, they can be so much more than just simple decorations. For this project I explore two different kinds of decoration: a wall hanging that consists of a swag of sculptural elements hung from a wooden branch; and a series of large, folded paper stars and snowflakes that can be arranged on a wall or hung in groups from the ceiling.

SWAG

This swag is a piece of decoration that doesn't need to be taken down. It has a sculptural quality that creates an array of shadows on the wall, yet is visually subtle using only whites and natural wood. It consists of hand-formed discs of different sizes made from polymer clay, a modelling material that hardens in the oven.

YOU WILL NEED

680 g (1½ lb) of white polymer clay, such as Skulpey

Small rolling pin

Small awl or nail to create a hole to fit the twine

Oven to harden the polymer clay

Baking tray

Baking paper

7.5 m (8 yd) of natural colour baker's twine/string

91.5 cm (36 in) wooden dowel or found branch, about 2.5 cm (1 in) in diameter

— I found that, when tying knots, if I place the point of my awl inside the knot, and close to the side of the disc, I can guide the knot to where I want it to be as I pull the string and it will tighten close to the hole.

— As you work, you can hold up your string of discs to get a feel for whether the length and spacing is appropriate for each tier. You can also pin each strand of knotted discs to the wall so you can decide how long to make each grouping.

Roll a small amount of polymer clay into a ball and then squish it flat with your fingers. A small rolling pin (I used a paper glue stick) will help to flatten out each disc. They do not have to be perfectly formed circles, and in fact some imperfections make them seem more organic. Make each disc no thinner than a coin – as you make them, you'll get a feel as to how thick you want them to be. Make a variety of diameters ranging from 2.5–6.5 cm (1–2½ in). I made 139 discs for my swag. With your awl, or a nail, punch a little hole in the centre of each disc only large enough to thread the twine you will be using without difficulty.

Arrange the clay discs spaced on a baking sheet lined with baking paper and bake them in the oven in batches, following the instructions on the packaging. Set aside to cool before continuing.

(1) To attach the discs onto the twine, I created 5 tiers of different lengths, each holding a different number of discs: tier 1 (16 discs), tier 2 (20 discs), tier 3 (24 discs), tier 4 (34 discs), and tier 5 (45 discs). Keep in mind that this project is open to interpretation so don't feel that you must replicate the one I made exactly. The lengths of your tiers will vary depending on how many discs you have and how you space them out – I spaced them somewhat randomly varying between 2.5 cm (1 in) to 6.5 cm (2½ in). Keep in mind that each disc will need a knot on either side to keep it in place (depending on the size of the hole you may need 2–3 knots on either side) and knots take a fair amount of twine, so cut the twine at least double the length, or more, to achieve the final length you want for each tier. If you do run out of twine you can create a magic knot – it's a good knot if you should need to add more length.

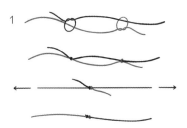

Start by cutting a length of twine for one of the tiers: determine visually how long you would like it to be, then double that measurement and add an additional 38 cm (15 in) on each end to tie it to the wood. Place the first disc by tying a knot, larger than the hole on the disc, about 38 cm (15 in) from one end of the twine. (2) Then slide a disc onto the twine up to the knot and tie another knot, snug next to it on the other side to prevent any movement. Repeat this for each disc, spacing them out accordingly. Repeat with each length of twine until you have as many strands as you wish.

Mount the dowel or branch about 4 cm (1½ in) away from the wall. There are many ways to do this, the simplest being to fix 2 small pieces of wood onto the wall, spaced accordingly, using screws and plugs if necessary. Then attach the dowel to the wood pieces with screws.

Attach your tiers to the dowel or branch by wrapping the twine around several times and tying with a knot. Arrange the tiers so that they attach to the wood at different locations and overlap each other as they hang.

TIPS

— If your tracing paper is particularly waxy, you may find it difficult to achieve a good bond. To test, fold two pieces of scrap tracing paper and test your glue by applying it to one fold and gluing the fold of the other piece. If the glue isn't holding, try applying a more generous amount.

— You can adapt the pattern for this ornament by changing the shape of the rounded end and also the length of the tracing paper pieces. Make a large group of flowers and hang them in the window or in a hallway. When they are against the light they will glow, and you can also put twinkly lights behind them.

LARGE PAPER FLOWER

The translucency of tracing paper gives these folded ornaments an ethereal look that reflects light; they are lovely when backlit from a window. It's also the perfect material as it folds well, keeps clean sharp edges and is easy to cut in many layers. This design has rounded edges, but you can also adjust the shape to make it look more angular.

YOU WILL NEED

Thin cardboard, such as a cereal box

Pencil

Paper scissors

10 pieces of tracing paper, each
   17.75 x 23 cm (7 x 9 in)

9 pieces of tracing paper, each
   15 x 19 cm (6 x 7½ in)

8 pieces of tracing paper, each
   10 x 10 cm (4 x 4 in)

Scrap tracing paper

Hot glue stick

Sewing needle and thread

61 cm (24 in) of light weight
   (115 g/¼ lb) fishing line

(1) Create templates in thin cardboard with a rounded bottom edge to fit each size of tracing paper piece, using the drawing as a guide. Using a pencil and the template, trace the shapes onto all the tracing paper pieces. Cut all the shapes out. For each piece, create accordion folds across parallel with the long side and with each fold 1 cm (⅜ in) wide.

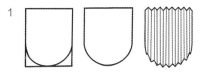

Once all pieces are folded, glue all the same-sized pieces together in a long line. Beginning with the large size, apply glue to the outside fold of one piece and join it to the outside fold of the next piece. Continue in this manner until all the large pieces are joined together, edge to edge, with the curves all on the same side. Once they are all glued together in a row, allow to dry while you repeat the same steps with the middle size and then the small size pieces.

(2) Thread the needle with an arm's length of thread and, beginning at the end of one long side of the large size pieces, pierce the centre of each fold about 1.25 cm (½ in) from the edge. The paper might be dense so pierce a few folds at a time. When your needle is at the opposite end and all folds have been threaded, remove the needle and adjust the thread so that there is at least 20–25 cm (8–10 in) of loose thread on each side.

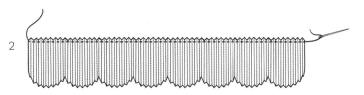

(3) Holding the thread ends, bring the ends together and tie them. Next, gently pull the ends until all the folds are cinched together and the centre is all tightly bundled in the middle of the shape. Tie it off using a double square knot. (4) The 2 remaining sides can now be glued together with hot glue, adding a length of fishing line through the glued folds near the outer edge to hang. You may need to place a light weight on the centre to keep the circle flat while you work on the other sized pieces. Repeat steps 3 and 4 for the 2 remaining sizes.

Once all circles are complete, glue all 3 layers together by applying a circle of hot glue to the centre area of the large circle and attaching the medium circle, making sure to keep both centred to each other. Joining the 2 circles together will give the paper flower more structure. Then repeat to glue the small circle onto the medium one.

4

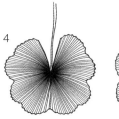
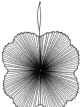

3

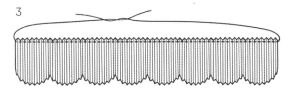

PAPER BAG SNOWFLAKES

Making paper snowflakes from kraft paper bags reminds me of my youth. They were so easy to make, but these ones are a definite step up – even though the method may be simple, these offer plenty of room for experimenting. You can easily modify their shape and heighten their visual impact by dyeing or painting your paper bags to play with colour and pattern. What I love about this project is that the ornaments are very quick to make with low material costs so if you don't plan to keep them, they can easily be recycled. I have included a few profile designs that you can use, but feel free to come up with your own.

YOU WILL NEED

12.5 x 7.5 x 25.5 cm (5 x 3 x 10 in) 7–8 brown kraft paper bags for each snowflake, each

Thin cardboard, such as a cereal box (optional)

Pencil

Paper scissors

Hot glue gun

0.5 cm (¼ in) hole punch

61 cm (24 in) of light weight (115 g/¼ lb) fishing line

(1) Flatten the first bag and draw your design at the opening end. You can use a template made from cardboard if you are making many, or you can use the first bag as your template for the remaining bags. Cut along the drawn line on all the paper bags.

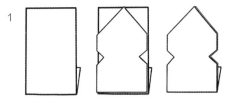

With the bags lying flat, you will notice that one side of the bag has the folded bottom/gusset while the other side is flat. Lay all the bags with flat side facing up – you will be applying glue on the flat side that has no flap. (2) If the design that you cut is symmetrical with both sides of the bag the same, then apply a line of glue down the centre of the bag from the bottom all the way to the cut line, and another along the bottom of the bag.

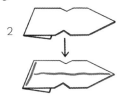

(3) If the design is cut asymmetrically so the bag has a front and a back, then apply a line of glue along the uncut edge from the bottom all the way to the top, and along the bottom as well.

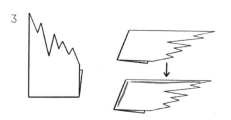

Apply the glue on the flat side of one bag and lay another bag on top, with all edges aligned and with the flat side facing up. Repeat until you have a stack with all the bags glued together.

(4) Open the shape up like you are opening a fan, apply glue to the last piece and attach it to the other side to form a complete circle. To hang the snowflake, punch a hole with a hole punch at the top of one of the glue lines where 2 bags are joined and tie a length of fishing line through.

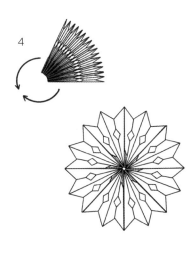

TIPS

— One of the ways I like to dye the paper is to create a water bath that is tall enough to dip the paper bag either half way or just the edge. You can add colour to the water bath by using acrylic paint or you can try using food colouring.

CUT PAPER STARS

This method of creating a paper star or snowflake is a combination of the previous two methods: the paper bag and accordion folded paper. I like this decoration because you can use wrapping paper, wallpaper or any kind of old paper from old magazines or books. This design will be a nice addition to the other two designs on pages 55 and 56.

YOU WILL NEED

10–13 sheets of any type of paper, each about
   11.5 x 30 cm (4½ x 12 in)

Ruler

Paper glue stick

Thin cardboard, such as a cereal box

Pencil

Scissors or rotary knife and cutting mat

Hot glue gun

Hole punch

38 cm (15 in) of string

— The scale of the paper pieces can vary with what you have on hand, but each piece should be rectangular so it can be folded in half.

(1) Fold each piece of paper lengthwise towards the centre on each side so that one flap is much wider than the other. For example, I folded one side of each piece over by 5 cm (2 in) on one side, and by 1 cm (⅜ in) on the other. Run the paper glue stick down the 1 cm (⅜ in) flap. Then, fold the 5 cm (2 in) flap over to stick in place and press firmly. The resulting shape will look like a flattened tube. Repeat for all the pieces. Press flat and let dry.

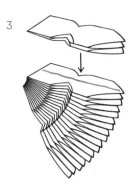

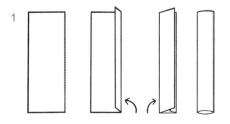

(2) Take each piece and fold in half lengthwise. Create a cardboard template the same size as the folded paper – mine was 5 x 15 cm (2 x 6 in), yours may differ depending on the size of your paper. Make cut-outs on each side and shape the end. Using a pencil, trace the template pattern onto each folded paper with the shaped end opposite the fold. Cut out the negative shapes using scissors or a rotary knife and cutting mat.

(4) Glue all the segments together by running a bead of hot glue down the centre of one segment and joining it to another until you make a complete circle. Be mindful as you glue to keep all edges aligned and the centre neat. Punch a hole near the outer edge along one of the glue lines to tie the string to hang your ornament.

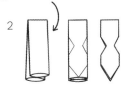

(3) Open each folded piece and put a bead of hot glue down the centre of the inside fold with a hot glue gun, and then fold back and press. When finished you will have triangular segments for your ornament.

Stands and Centrepieces

The centre of a table is often reserved for a bouquet. As much as I love fresh flowers, I have always been attracted to dried plants and botanical samples. My work has always had botanical references and I love collecting samples while out walking, which I display on a wall in my studio. They have a sculptural quality – a garden of shapes and details with imperfections that seem even more natural. Centrepieces made of sticks, grasses or interesting stems are perfect to create a tablescape with a natural theme and the delicate beauty of a winter garden. The plant matter you choose can be anything and there are many options for display; a collection of pieces can be larger or smaller depending on the size of your table, or single pieces for a more intimate setting.

YOU WILL NEED

Offcuts or small pieces of wood in different
  shapes, each at least 4–5 cm (1½–2 in) wide
Sandpaper
Pencil
Drill with a 3 mm (⅛ in) drill bit
Dried plant and flower stems

TIPS

— This tablescape consists of different shapes of wood as supports for plant matter. There are a variety of sizes and heights that can be reconfigured to different shapes, sizes and orientations. I used similar offcuts of wood that I had on hand, all of which had a slight angle so they appear almost like a landscape. You can use pieces that are quite different to each other, if you prefer.

— When drilling make sure that you have the block of wood secured and clamped down. Drill each hole down vertically so that the plant stands upright regardless of the shape of the block. I used a 3 mm (⅛ in) drill bit, which seemed adequate for the plants I was using; you might need to use a larger drill bit if necessary.

Give the wood shapes a few rounded corners with the sandpaper to give them a slightly finished look.

With a pencil, mark where you want holes for the stems. Space the holes as you wish, leaving enough space between each hole for the plants to spread. I left about 4–5 cm (1½–2 in) between each hole. Keep the position of the holes random so it seems organic.

Drill each hole about 5 cm (2 in) deep, or as deep as possible on smaller blocks.

Take your dried plant and flower stems and start adding them to the wood blocks, trimming the stems if necessary. You can find stems at a florists, but I prefer ones that I have collected from gardens and parks. Use a variety of shapes and sizes to create movement across the arrangement and also play with the heights.

Arrange the blocks in loose rows with a little space between them. This can also be done on a smaller scale if you want to decorate a small table in a hallway or on a mantle. If so, use a smaller number of blocks, or just a single shaped block drilled with several holes.

Gift

Wrapping

The first thing you see when receiving a gift is the wrapping. And while typically quite decorative, it can be a bit of an afterthought. But there are many thoughtful ways to heighten the experience of opening a gift. One of my favourites is to make wrapping paper by block printing a repeat pattern. I like the simplicity of kraft paper to highlight images that I have designed, but you can use other papers or even recycled paper. You can also make reusable wrapping with cloth, where the wrapping itself becomes part of the gift. Again, you can print your own design if you like or use fabric that you have on hand.

WRAPPING CLOTH

Creating a reusable wrapping cloth, known as furoshiki, means you will be giving two presents in one: the cloth itself and the contents. It's the perfect way to avoid creating any waste by making wrapping that is actually useful. To make it special, this cloth is eco-painted with a unique design, first by painting soy milk onto the surface, and then dyeing it with botanical items from your kitchen such as avocado pits, onion skins and coffee or tea.

YOU WILL NEED

4 x 53.5 x 53.5 cm (21 x 21 in) of cotton or other natural fabric

125 ml (4 fl oz) of soy milk

Measuring cup

1 tablespoon of guar gum

Spatula for mixing

Piece of paper, slightly larger than the fabric

Masking tape

Water-soluble fabric marker

No. 16 round brush

2.5 cm (1 in) wide flat brush

Scrap fabric

Pins (optional)

Drying rack (optional)

Kitchen scraps, such as avocado pits and skins, onion skins, pomegranate skins

Pot for the dye mix, large enough to hold the fabric

Mixing spoons for the dye mix

Used coffee grounds

Tea bag

Heat source, such as a hob

Mild laundry detergent

Sewing machine and matching thread

Iron

TIPS

— The final size of this wrapping will be around 51 x 51 cm (20 x 20 in), but feel free to create a larger or smaller size that suits your gifting needs.

—The soy milk mixture is enough to paint five pieces of 53.5 x 53.5 cm (21 x 21 in) cloth.

— You can paint soy milk onto fabric without adding guar gum, but you will have more bleeding and less control over where it goes.

— When you are naturally dyeing at home it's good to have designated pots and utensils that don't mix with food cooking. Even though these materials are not corrosive or toxic, it's good practice to not mix the two. You can find pots at charity shops or thrift store.

— I made four different colours, one for each piece of fabric, using coffee, avocado seeds and skins, onion skins, and pomegranate skins. Use whatever you have on hand.

Depending on the size of the item you are wrapping you can cut your fabric to be larger or smaller. I found that 53.5 x 53.5 cm (21 x 21 in) is a good average size to go with. I cut 4 pieces to be dyed with 4 different natural dyes.

The soy milk will act as a binder when applied to areas of fabric; when the fabric is dyed those areas will appear darker and more intense compared to areas without any soy milk applied. Add the soy milk to the measuring cup and slowly add the guar gum while stirring with the spatula. As you add the guar gum you will notice the mixture thickening – stop adding guar gum when the consistency is like thin yoghurt. This will allow the soy mixture to be applied with a brush. Continue to stir to remove any lumps. It is best to use the mixture soon after you mix it.

Place the fabric on top of a piece of paper and tape the 4 corners to prevent it from moving. Using the water-soluble marker, draw a design of your choice onto the fabric. Before you start painting, test your brush strokes on a scrap piece of fabric to get a feel for how much of the soy milk mixture you should put on your brush. When you are ready, paint all areas of your design, ensuring that each shape is thoroughly wetted. Try to keep your designs simple without too many fine details, such as geometric shapes. They can be placed randomly or in more structured compositions, it's completely up to you.

Once you finish painting, pin the fabric to a wall or hang on a drying rack. The soy milk should be left to cure for 3–5 days; the longer you let it sit the stronger the colour will be. As the fabric dries it will stiffen up in the painted areas and you will notice a thin coating has become visible.

Prepare each dye bath separately by adding a handful of dry materials into the pot and covering with water – the more dry material you add the stronger the colour will be. Heat until boiling then turn down and let simmer for about an hour. Once you start seeing colour in the water, remove all plant material and filter out the coffee grounds, if using. Slowly submerge each piece of dry fabric into the liquid. Increase the heat and gently boil for about an hour before turning the heat off and leaving to soak in the liquid overnight. The next day, rinse the fabric and wash by hand using a mild detergent. Hang to dry.

Sew a rolled hem around all 4 edges of the fabric by turning the edge of the fabric under by 1.25 cm (½ in) twice so that the raw edges are folded inside. Use a sewing machine to sew all around the edge of the fold. Press the fabric.

Place your present in the centre of the cloth, fold it over and tie knots with the opposite corners. The reusable wrapping will not only be holding the gift but can also be a gift to in itself. It can be used as scarf, a tea towel or handkerchief.

BLOCK-PRINTED PAPER

This project is a good way to reuse any lino blocks that you may have leftover from other projects. Designs that you carve into the blocks can be flowers or snowflakes with added details, or simple geometric or random shapes. And they can be printed in various colours on any type of paper – it's really up to you. I like to use kraft paper because of its durability and utilitarian look. When tied with a ribbon or yarn your paper will look like pieces of art that will definitely stand out.

YOU WILL NEED

Soft linoleum block

No. 3 nib lino cutting tool, or any size of your preference

White bond or kraft paper or similar

Masking tape

White, black and gold water-based block printing ink

Aluminium rolling tray or Styrofoam

Foam roller

Baren (optional)

If you don't already have a lino block to use, draw a design of your choice onto the lino and cut out the negative spaces – the areas you don't want to print. Place your paper on a table and tape down all 4 corners securely to prevent it moving.

Tip a small amount of ink onto the tray and roll with the foam roller until the roller has an even coat of ink. Roll the ink onto the carved side of the block. Make sure to give the design a thin, even coat of ink, and keep in mind that when printing on paper you don't need a lot of ink as it can smudge when you press down.

Place the block onto the paper where you desire and push down onto the paper with the ink side down. I like to use a baren because it helps me get a print with even pressure, but if you don't have one just use your fingertips and push all around the block to give it even pressure. Try not to push down with your palm as this can push the block forward, causing the image to smudge. Once you are done printing leave the paper to dry completely before wrapping your gift.

— I used white, black and gold block printing inks but you can use any colours you like.
— As an alternative to the lino block you can carve your design into the cut surface of a halved potato.

— Try to print your image randomly and keep in mind the types of gifts you will be wrapping. For example, for a small object you might want your placement to be closer and for a larger object, you will want it further apart.

SMALL DRAWSTRING BAG

This round drawstring bag makes for a really lovely way to wrap small items and the bag itself is also reusable for other purposes. You can use fabric that you already have on hand and some twill tape and ribbon. It doesn't take long to make and finishes off the gift beautifully.

YOU WILL NEED

28 cm (11 in), 33 cm (13 in) and 46 cm (18 in) diameter circles of outer fabric

28 cm (11 in), 33 cm (13 in) and 46 cm (18 in) diameter circles of calico (cotton muslin) or similar lining fabric

81.25 cm (32 in) of 1.25 cm (½ in) twill tape or ribbon for each bag

Snips and scissors

Sewing machine and matching thread

91.5 cm (36 in) of 1.25 cm (½ in) twill tape or ribbon for each bag

TIPS

— This design can be adapted to any scale depending on what you will need to wrap. The three sizes I made are 28 cm (11 in), 33 cm (13 in) and 46 cm (18 in) in diameter.
— For my smallest size I spaced the 16 tabs about 5 cm (2 in) apart; for the medium size the 16 tabs were spaced about 6.5 cm (2½ in) apart; for the largest size the 16 tabs were spaced about 9 cm (3½ in) apart.

(1) For each bag you will need one circle of fabric for the outside and one for the lining. Cut the 81.25 cm (32 in) of 1.25 cm (½ in) length of twill tape or ribbon into 5 cm (2 in) lengths. You will need 16 pieces for each bag.

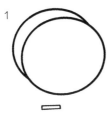

(2) Start by sewing the drawstring tabs around the perimeter of the good side of the outer fabric. To do this, fold each length of twill tape or ribbon in half and place around the perimeter of the circle with the fold pointing inwards toward the centre and the ends aligned with the outer edge. Tack down close to the edge with the sewing machine.

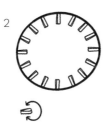

(3) Place the lining circle on the outer fabric with right sides together and the outer edge aligned (the tabs will be hidden in between the layers). Sew around the edge using a 1 cm (⅜ in) seam allowance leaving an unsewn opening between 2 of the tabs.

Snip small triangles into the seam allowance all around the edge so that it will have a nice curve. Taking care not to cut any of the tabs. (4) Turn right side out through the unsewn opening and fold in the edges of the opening. Top stitch (see page 13) all around close to the edge – this will also close the opening.

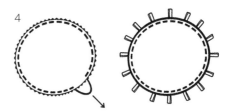

(5) Thread the 91.5 cm (36 in) length of twill tape or ribbon through all the tabs. Place your present in the centre, cinch the ribbon closed, and tie into a bow.

Woven Pouch

What makes this pouch distinctive is the woven front panel, which can be different every time you make it. The unique quality of weaving with different colours gives the piece a textured pattern that is equally playful and elegant. And this type of weaving doesn't need any sort of frame – just pins to hold the strips of fabric in place – so it is incredibly quick and easy. I used five different colours of cotton quilting weight fabric, but you can easily use any fabric that you have on hand, solids or prints.

YOU WILL NEED

Cotton or similar lightweight fabric in 5 different colours, each piece about 12.5 x 60 cm (5 x 24 in)

Rotary cutter and cutting mat (optional)

Clear ruler

Pencil

Scissors

Bias tape maker to make 1.25 cm (½ in) strips

Iron

Foam sheet larger than 32 x 21.5 cm (12½ x 8½ in)

Pins

Weft weaving tool

Masking tape

32 x 21.5 cm (12½ x 8½ in) of fusible (iron on) non-woven interfacing

28 cm (11 in) metal zipper

2 pieces of calico (cotton muslin) lining, each 32 x 21.5 cm (12½ x 8½ in)

32 x 21.5 cm (12½ x 8½ in) of cotton backing fabric

Wooden toggle or bead

Short length of leather or fabric cord

Cut the fabric into strips 2.5 cm (1 in) wide using a rotary cutter and clear ruler. If you don't have those tools, mark the fabric with a ruler and a pencil and cut with scissors. Do not cut the lengths yet. I used 5 different reds, yellows and pinks in various tints.

Use the bias tape maker to fold the edges of the strips under by feeding the strips through the large opening and slowly pulling them out the smaller opening. If you can, follow along the bias tape maker with an iron to flatten the folds. You will end up with a 1.25 cm (½ in) strip with edges folded under giving you a clean edge. Repeat for all of the fabric strips.

The warp has 5 strips of each colour, for a total of 25 strips, each 25 cm (10 in) long. The weft has 3 strips each of 3 colours and 4 strips each of the other 2 colours, for a total of 17 strips, each 36 cm (14 in) long. Cut all the strips to length.

(1) Place the foam sheet on your worktable and lay the weft strips on top in horizontal rows with ends aligned. Lay out the strips with the 5 colours in the order that you want them to appear and then repeat that order until all 17 strips form a height of 21.5 cm (8½ in). At the end of each strip place a pin on an angle into the foam to hold each strip in place. Make sure that the strips are pulled taut when placing the second pin.

For the vertical warp rows, I kept the pattern of the colours the same. (2) Start your weaving on one side and, using the weft tool to help guide the warp strips, weave by going under and over each of the horizontal weft strips. If you like you can temporarily pin the horizontal strips to keep them from moving – I pinned about every 4 strips to start, and fewer as the weaving progressed. Try to make sure that the strips are tightly woven and the whole panel is kept square.

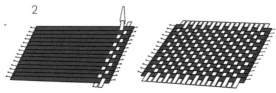

When the weaving is finished, place a line of masking tape on top of the panel, along the edge of all 4 sides, removing the pins as you go. (3) Turn the panel over and iron the interfacing, with the glue side down, onto the back. Flip it over and carefully remove the masking tape. Press the top to make sure everything adheres well. Sew a top stitch (see page 13) close to the edge, along all 4 sides of the area that is completely woven – it should be an area of 32 x 21.5 cm (12½ x 8½ in) – and cut off all the strip ends that are outside that sewn line.

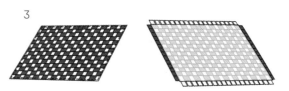

(4) Lay the zipper, facing up, on top of one of the lining pieces, also right side up, so that the zipper is centred and aligned along the long top edge. Next, lay the woven front piece, right side down, on top of the zipper, again with the long top edge aligned with the zipper and lining below. Using a zipper foot, stitch along the edge with a 1 cm (⅜ in) seam allowance.

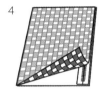

(5) Fold over the woven panel and lining to expose the other, unfinished edge of the zipper. Repeat the above steps by placing the zipper, facing up, on top of the right side of the other piece of lining, centred and aligned along the long top edge, then place the backing fabric, right side down, on top of the zipper also centred and aligned along the top long edge. Using a zipper foot, stitch along the edge with a 1 cm (⅜ in) seam allowance.

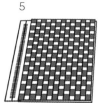

Lay the pouch flat with the 2 linings on top of each other on one side of the zipper and the front and back of the pouch on the other, both with right sides facing.

(6) Sew the front and back panels together along all 3 unsewn sides with a 1 cm (⅜ in) seam, then sew a 2.5 cm (1 in) gusset across each corner. Sew the 2 pieces of lining together, sewing along all 3 sides with a 1 cm (⅜ in) seam allowance but leaving a 7.5 cm (3 in) unsewn gap midway in the long bottom edge to turn right sides out. Finish the lining by sewing a 2.5 cm (1 in) gusset across each lining corner.

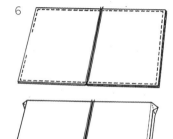

Reach into the unsewn gap, open the zipper and pull right sides out. Stitch the opening in the lining closed with your machine, or by hand with a whip stitch (see page 16), and then push the lining inside the pouch. If necessary, you can press the pouch with an iron.

Add a wooden toggle or bead to the short length of leather or fabric cord and tie it to the zipper pull.

Small Patchwork Pouch

Patchwork is one of my favourite ways of making bags and personal items. Even the smallest of pouches can have a modern and artisanal look. These curved pouches are made from fabric remnants and are quite versatile – the added wristlet makes them so easy to wear as a wallet, but they are equally useful as a pouch for all your odds and ends to help keep your bag or luggage organized. I begin patching in an improvisational way – I don't have a specific pattern or intention in mind, which makes the process very freeing.

YOU WILL NEED

Selection of fabric remnants in assorted colours

Sewing machine with thread to coordinate with fabric colours

Template on page 155

Pencil

Scissors

15 x 20 cm (6 x 8 in) of linen fabric for the back (optional)

30 x 20 cm (12 x 8 in) of cotton twill lining fabric

23 cm (9 in) metal zipper

Pins

33 cm (⅜ x 13 in) leather strip for wristlet

Rivet hole punch

Rivet

Hammer

TIPS

— The finished size of patchwork should be 14 x 17 cm (5½ x 6¾ in) for the front panel, and the same size for the back panel if this will be patchwork also.

— If you don't have a leather strip you can either sew a strip of fabric or use a short length of thin rope for the wristlet.

With your remnants organized into colours, choose one to start with and use the shape of your remnants to guide the direction of how the patchwork develops. Adding one piece at a time, and joining with 1 cm (⅜ in) seam allowances, gradually build up the patchwork, rotating as you go and adding colours. I try to keep the seams matched up so that it gives it a more organized feel. Continue working until you have a piece large enough to cover the template (2 pieces if you are patching both sides of the pouch).

Copy the template provided to size – keep in mind that you will have to reverse it when cutting out the back panel so the curve is correct for both the front and back panels. If you are not using patchwork for the back, cut the back from the piece of linen. Also use the template to cut 2 pieces of the twill for the lining.

(1) Switch to a zipper foot on your sewing machine. I like to have the beginning of the zipper to be on the top (short side) of the pouch – start sewing the zipper here. With the patchwork panel right side up, place the start of the zipper (where the pull is when it is closed) on top of the front panel, facing down, aligned at the corner and along the top edge. On top of the zipper place one of

the lining pieces, right side down, aligned with the patchwork panel below so the zipper is in between. Starting at the corner, sew all 3 layers together along the edge with a 1 cm (⅜ in) seam allowance.

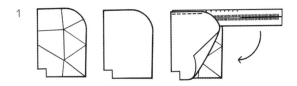

(2) As you reach the curve, use your scissors to periodically snip along the edge of the zipper, going in about 0.25cm (⅛ in) – this will help the zipper bend a little as you pin it around the curve. Continue sewing down along the long side to the bottom corner. When finished, snip little darts in the seam allowance along the curve to give it a nicer shape.

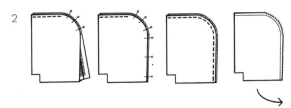

(3) Fold both panels away from the zipper to expose the unsewn edge of the zipper. Add the back panel right side facing the patchwork panel and add the lining right side facing the other lining piece with all aligned on the unsewn zipper edge. Sew the edge as in steps 3 and 4 with a 1 cm (⅜ in) seam allowance, snipping the zipper edge along the curve and when finished cutting darts into the seam allowance where the pouch curves.

3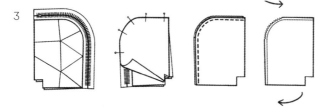

(4) To close the pouch, place the front and back panels of the pouch right sides together with the edges aligned, and pin. Then place the 2 pieces of lining right sides together and edges aligned, and pin. Align the seams where the zipper starts and ends and pin or tack down with a sewing machine.

4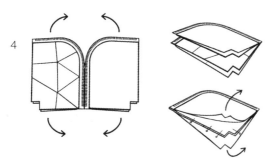

(5) Sew the 2 linings together and the 2 outside panels together around the curve and along the straight bottom edge only using a 1 cm (⅜ in) seam allowance. Leave a 5 cm (2 in) gap in one side to turn the pouch right side out – do not sew around the cut-out corners.

5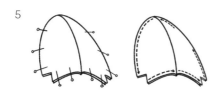

(6) Pull each corner out until the cut-out makes a straight line and sew along the line to create a gusset across both bottom corners of the lining and the outside panels.

6

(7) Turn the pouch right side out through the opening in the seam. Make sure to push into the corner of the outer panels out so that it will be nice and square. Sew the opening in the lining seam closed and then push the lining back inside the pouch.

7

(8) On one end of the thin leather strip punch a hole 0.5 cm (¼ in) from the end and on the other end fold the leather over by 3 cm (1¼ in) and punch another hole through both layers 0.5 cm (¼ in) from the end. Attach the wristlet strap by opening out the folded end and threading it through the zipper pull until the zipper pull sits on the fold line. Then fold over again and place the other end of the strap inside the fold so that all 3 holes align. Place a rivet inside the hole and hammer closed.

8

Leaf Relief Printed Pouch

It's impossible not to find inspiration in nature. Plants, leaves and flowers have always been reference material for the surface designs I use when making textile goods. But botanical samples can also be used as materials to work with, especially when printing. Despite being delicate, leaves and flowers are perfect for relief printing. When used on small items like pouches, they can lend a real beauty that captures shapes and forms in such detail. And because they are so easy to print, any interesting find from a walk or your garden is a design just waiting to happen.

YOU WILL NEED

Leaves or flowers (dried and fresh)

Cotton fabric remnants in various sizes or colours

25 cm (¼ yd) of calico (cotton muslin) fabric for the lining

Ruler or tape measure

Scissors

Fabric ink

Spoon

Plate for ink

2.5cm (1 in) diameter sponge stencil brush with wooden handle

Pieces of scrap paper

Iron

15 cm (6 in), 23 cm (9 in) and 25 cm (10 in) metal or plastic zippers

30 cm (12 in) leather cord

2 cm (¾ in) wooden bead

TIPS

— Pressing flowers or composite leaves flat will create a better and more complete printed image, but they can become brittle over time and break while printing. You can work with fresh plants for longer because they are more flexible and durable and they are full of details, but sometimes they can be too three-dimensional for a flat print.

— These pouches range in size from 15 cm (6 in) to 25 cm (10 in) wide, but the pattern can be altered to fit any size or shape so any cotton fabric remnants that you may have will do.

Collect a variety of plants, leaves and flowers. Both fresh and pressed plants can be used for printing, but some experimentation might be necessary to find the best method depending on the plants you chose. For these pouches I used dried plants. Choose which plants you want to use and cut both your fabric and lining into pairs of rectangles the desired size for your pouch. You can print one side of your pouch or both sides.

Spread a spoonful of ink on the plate and blot with the sponge brush, making sure to get an even coat of ink on the brush. Place the leaf/flower on scrap paper, holding it down by its stem, and gently blot ink on the surface making sure it's even all over. Pick the leaf/flower up by the stem and place it ink side down onto the cotton fabric. Carefully cover it with a piece of paper larger than the print and gently rub all over making sure to press all areas. Remove the paper and pick up the leaf/flower to reveal the print.

If the plant matter is not too fragile it can be used multiple times to make additional prints or to create a repeat pattern. Make sure to use a fresh piece of paper for each print. Once the ink dries, cover with a scrap piece of fabric and press with an iron on the top and back for a few minutes. This will set the ink and make it colour fast.

(1) Lay the zipper right side up on top of one of the lining pieces so that it is centred and aligned along the long top edge. Lay the printed front piece, right side down, on top of the zipper, again with the long top edge aligned with the zipper and lining below. Using a zipper foot, stitch along the edge with a 1 cm (⅜ in) seam allowance. Fold over the printed front and lining away from the zipper.

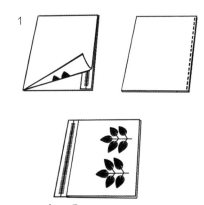

(2) Repeat the previous step on the other side of the zipper with the lining right side up centred underneath the unsewn zipper edge and the second printed piece right side down on top of the zipper, with all layers aligned along the top edge. Using a zipper foot, stitch along the edge with a 1 cm (⅜ in) seam allowance.

(4) After turning right sides out, pull the lining out and stitch the opening closed with the machine or by hand with a whip stitch (see page 16), and then push the lining back inside. If necessary, you can press the pouch with an iron. Lastly add the leather cord with the wooden bead to the zipper pull.

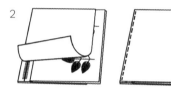

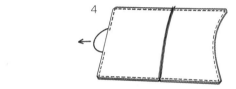

(3) Lay the pouch flat with the 2 linings right sides facing on top of each other on one side of the zipper and the front and back of the pouch right sides facing on the other side of the zipper. Sew around the perimeter on all sides of both the outer pieces and the linings with a 1 cm (⅜ in) seam, leaving a 7.5 cm (3 in) unsewn opening on the long side of the lining to turn right sides out. Clip across all 4 corners of the fabric before turning out.

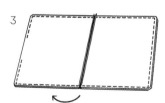

Simple Mitts

Mittens are a necessary part of your life if you live within winter's reach. And a handmade pair, quite often knitted, can be both a prized possession and a welcome gift. This project is a slightly different take on handmade mitts and is so quick and simple it can be done in under 30 mins. It is made of remnants of old knitted sweaters and, since the pattern is made of four distinct sections, it is a nice way to play with different colours, textures or patterns. I made a set of four pairs using four different colours with different combinations for each.

YOU WILL NEED

Templates on page 156–157

Pieces of knitted fabric from a sweater

Water-soluble fabric marker

Scissors

Pins

Sewing machine and thread
 to coordinate with fabrics

Ruler

Sewing needle

Top stitch quilting thread

— I like to wash the fabric on a high temperature before using it – washing knitted sweater makes them somewhat felted and denser, which will make them less airy and warmer. I used a cashmere wool for my mitts.
— When you are sewing knitwear there is a lot of stretch, so pinning the pieces will prevent movement.

— The design consists of four sections: top palm (A), bottom palm (B), back of hand (C) and wrist (D). You will need two of pieces A, B and C (one for each hand) and four of piece D (two for each hand).

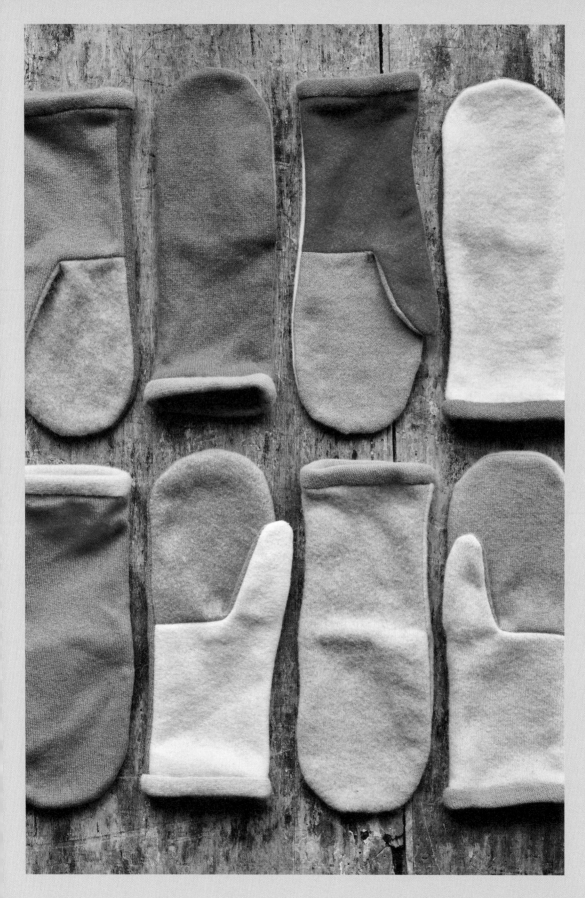

Copy the template to size and use the water-soluble marker to trace the design onto pieces of knitted fabric. Remember to mark the little line shown on pieces A and B with a notch or pin. When you trace the 2 palm pieces, remember to flip them over for the second set so they will work for both the left and right hands. This is important if the sweater has a pattern or if you want to show the right side of the fabric. Cut around the drawn lines.

(1) Start by placing the top and bottom section of the palm side right sides together (pieces A and B), aligning edges. Sew together using a 1 cm (⅜ in) seam allowance, only along the straight edge to the thumb then pivoting at the corner and continuing around the thumb, stopping at the marked line. Take the scissors and cut small darts around the tip of the thumb and a snip at the corner of the thumb. Fold the top section of the palm upwards.

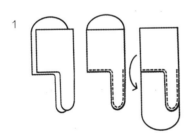

(2) Place the sewn section on top of the back of the hand (piece C) of the mitt with right sides together. Using a 1 cm (⅜ in) seam allowance, sew from the bottom edge to where the seam stopped at the base of the thumb in step 2. Then fold the thumb over

out of the way and sew from this point all around the curve and down to the bottom edge again, leaving the opening for the hand unsewn. Cut darts around the curve of the mitt and turn it right side out.

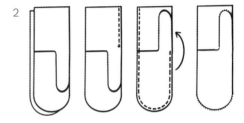

(3) Take 2 pieces of D, which make the bias for the wrist, and sew the short edges on both sides together using a 1 cm (⅜ in) seam allowance. Slide the cuff over to the bottom edge of a mitt with right sides together so the bottom edge is aligned with the bottom edge of the mitt. Make sure to line up the seams and pin in place. Sew around the edge, attaching the 2 layers together, using a 1.5 cm (⅝ in) seam allowance.

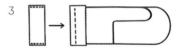

(4) Fold down the unsewn edge into the inside of the mitt. Thread the needle with the top stitching thread and tie a quilter's knot (see page 15) at one end. Use a whip stitch (see page 16) to sew all around the raw inside edge to finish the wrist. Repeat steps 2 to 5 for the second mitt.

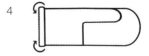

Printed Tea Towel

Every kitchen needs tea towels and the nicest ones usually hang in a noticeable spot, which makes them a perfect gift for anyone who loves useful items that are also lovely to look at. And making tea towels with your own personalized design is quite easy. I love the look of block printing combined with the natural quality of linen; with even the simplest of shapes and patterns, these prints will elevate any kitchen.

YOU WILL NEED

Template on page 155

White paper

Soft dark pencil

Soft linoleum block

Spoon

No. 3 nib lino cutting tool, or any size of your preference

White bond or kraft paper or similar

46 x 63.5 cm (18 x 25 in) of linen or cotton for each tea towel

Masking tape

Fabric ink in various colours

Aluminium rolling tray, Styrofoam or piece of plexiglass

Foam roller

Baren (optional)

Iron

Old pillowcase or piece of scrap fabric

Pin

10 cm (4 in) of 1.25 cm (½ in) wide twill tape for each tea towel

Sewing machine and matching thread

TIPS

— The finished tea towel is 43.5 x 61 cm (17 x 24 in) with a 1.25 cm (½ in) rolled hem all around, or you can purchase pre-made tea towels to print onto.
— If you're making multiple tea towels from fabric, cut them all to size first – it's best to do each step for all towels at once. As an alternative to the lino block you can carve your design into the cut surface of halved a potato.

— With individual images I tend to create random patterns across the surface when printing, but for images that are more structured, such as the curves or triangles, I tend to join them together to make a larger pattern. But feel free to find your own way and have fun with it.

(1) Copy any motifs of your choice from the template to your desired size onto paper. Then, using a soft dark pencil, retrace over the image. This will create a carbon effect so that you can transfer the image onto the soft linoleum block. Place the image drawing side down onto the block and, using the back of a spoon, rub the back of the paper until the image transfers to the block. At this point the image will be backwards so that when you print it will appear correct.

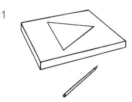

(2) Use the lino cutting tool to carve the design into the block, removing all the areas that are negative spaces – the areas that will be white/background with no design. Make sure to go deep enough so the white areas will not get inked but not too deep – if you go too shallow the ink will pool into the cut-out areas and if you go too deep that might compromise the shape of the block, making it not print properly.

(3) Cut off an excess area around the design. Cover your worktable to protect it and place your tea towel fabric on top. Tape down the tea towel on all 4 corners to prevent it from moving.

Tip some ink into the rolling tray or plexiglass. Roll into the ink, back and forth, with the foam roller until you have an even surface and it's not too thick or blobby. It's best to do a test print to make sure that you are using a good amount of ink before printing on your tea towel.

(4) Roll the ink onto the carved side of the block. When printing on fabric you want to be generous with the ink so it makes a good impression. Press the inked block onto the tea towel with the ink side down using a baren or your fingertips and push all around the block for even pressure. Try not to push down with your palm as the block might move and smudge the image. Reapply ink to the block every time you make a print.

After the print dries, heat-set it by running an iron over it for 2–3 minutes on high heat with no steam. Place an old pillowcase or scrap fabric on top of the printed area when ironing the front to prevent any smudging.

Fold the fabric edge under to the wrong side by 0.5 cm (¼ in) twice and press. Fold the twill tape in half and tuck the raw ends into the hem on one of the top corners on an angle to create a hanging hoop, and pin to secure. With your sewing machine, top stitch to secure the hem and the hanging loop in place, starting at a corner and stitching along all 4 edges.

Painted Ceramics

Ceramics are works of art that make great gifts. To make them in the traditional way takes a fair amount of commitment to the craft, but there are options to use ceramic paint and pens that have real decorative possibilities. They allow for a personal expression that is very similar to the tradition of glazing pots with drawings, motifs or patterns, but makes the experience of decorating ceramics completely accessible. All you need is a regular oven and ready-made ceramic pieces, which can be found at any second-hand shop or thrift sore, kitchen supply or home decor store.

YOU WILL NEED

Water-soluble marker

White pots or vases in various shapes and sizes

Paper (optional)

Masking tape (optional)

Size 0.7 and 1.2 ceramic pens in Lapis

Oven to set the ceramic paint

TIPS

— I favour a matte look so when selecting pots I lean toward a non-glossy finish, but this is a personal preference, either will work fine.
— I use Pebeo ceramic pens. The Pebeo brand also makes a ceramic paint in liquid form but I find it easier to use the pens for more graphic designs. If you want your work to be more painterly then the paint version is good for you.
— When painting your design it's good to go with more simple shapes and patterns with thick lines rather than something more refined and detailed.

Start by using a water-soluble marker to map out your design onto your vase or pot. You can also use masking tape and paper to block off areas you want to be protected.

Draw over your design using a ceramic pen. I used the fine size 0.7 to do an outline first before filling in any areas with the thicker 1.2 marker. You may have to go over some areas twice to get a solid uniform colour. Since the marker is not permanent before it's cured in the oven, you can remove areas that you have drawn if you change your mind or make a mistake by soaking the piece in water (although you may still get a bit of staining). It's best to work in sections and let each section dry before moving on to the next area, to avoid smudging while handling the piece as you work.

After you finish painting, set the pot or vase aside to fully dry for 24 hours. Then, place it in your oven to cure the ceramic paint so that it will be permanent and can be washed. Heat for 35 minutes at 150°C (300°F), in a domestic oven (please refer to the pen manufacturer's instructions for detailed instructions). Remove from the oven and set to cool.

Eco Washcloth

This is the kind of gift that we all need. A washcloth for the kitchen is certainly useful, but what makes this one even better is that it is made from old T-shirts eco-dyed with plant material from your kitchen. It can easily be washed and used over and over. Weaving the fabric takes only a simple homemade frame and is fast enough that you can make several in no time at all. A couple would be nice as a set gifted with a bar of soap.

YOU WILL NEED

25 x 25 cm (10 x 10 in) wooden board, 2 cm (¾ in) thick

Ruler

Pencil

34 nails approx. 4 cm (1½ in) long

Hammer

Pots for the dye mix

Mixing spoons for the dye mix

Kitchen scraps, such as avocado pits and skins, onion skins, pomegranate skins

Heat source, such as a hob

3 or 4 old T-shirts

Mild laundry detergent

Rotary cutter and cutting mat (optional)

Scissors

Tapestry needle

TIPS

— Each washcloth uses two different colours dyed from either avocado seeds and skins, onion skins or pomegranate skins. But feel free to use whatever natural dye material you have on hand.

— Make sure when you are creating the warp that you keep the fabric strip taut to keep the weave tight and prevent any sagging.

— The length of your strips will not be long enough to complete the entire warp so you will have to join smaller lengths as you go. I typically hand sew the ends of strips together, but you can also tie the ends together and work the knot into the weaving, or you can make a little slit at the ends of the two strips to be joined and loop one end through the other.

— To add additional lengths to the weft you can weave about 5 cm (2 in) of a new strip layered on top of 5 cm (2 in) of the tail from the previous strip.

Start by making a frame on which to weave the washcloth. Draw a square measuring 20 x 20 cm (8 x 8 in) onto the piece of wood. Starting at one corner, hammer nails every 1.25 cm (½ in) along one side of the square until you reach the other corner. Leave about 2.5 cm (1 in) of the nail above the surface. Repeat on the opposite side of the square, leaving the other 2 sides empty.

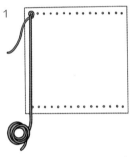

Prepare each dye bath separately by adding a handful of dry materials into the pot and cover with water – the more dry material you add the stronger the colour will be. Heat until boiling then turn down and let simmer for about an hour. You will start seeing colour in the water, so remove all plant material. Slowly submerge the dry fabric into the liquid. Increase the heat and gently boil for about an hour before turning the heat off and leaving to soak in the liquid overnight. The next day, rinse the fabric and wash by hand using a mild detergent. Hang to dry.

Cut the T-shirt fabric into 2.5 cm (1 in) strips; it's quick to do this with a ruler and rotary cutter, but if you don't have these tools you can just cut with the scissors. Accuracy in cutting the strips is not important, so you can do this free hand. The strips may also be various lengths. Once you cut the strips, pull on the fabric ends and you will notice the cut edges of the strips curl a little and appear almost rope-like.

(1) Start with any colour of strips you wish – I used one colour for the warp and a second colour for the weft. Tie a strip for the warp onto the first nail in the upper left-hand corner, leaving a tail of about 10 cm (4 in), which you will use to make a loop to hang the cloth. Create the warp with a continuous strip, wrapping around a nail on one side, then across to a nail on the other side then back again. Continue back and forth, until all the strip is wrapped around all the nails, then tie the end onto the last nail on the opposite corner diagonal to where you started.

Now start to weave the weft using a different colour. Starting at the same corner where you started the warp, tie the strip onto the first nail, again leaving a tail of about 10 cm (4 in). (2) Thread the fabric strip into your tapestry needle and begin weaving into the warp by going under and over, from one side to the other, then back again in an opposite over under motion.

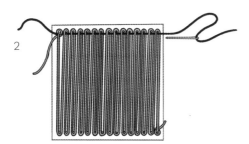

(3) Repeat, back and forth, row by row. Don't pull each row very tight to allow the weaving to remain square. As you complete each row push it against the previous row to keep the weave from becoming too loose. Finish off the weft by tying the end to the last nail and weaving the tail back into the piece.

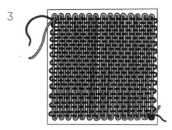

(4) Make a loop for hanging the cloth by tying the 2 tails together that you left from the start. Make the loop as big as you need. Slide the woven piece off the nails to finish.

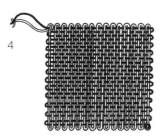

Appliqué Device Sleeve

This is a project for everyone. Not just because everyone has a laptop or tablet that could use a little protection, but because not everyone has such homemade style for their high technology. And why not? With its modern design of appliqué shapes and playful colours, this quilted sleeve makes for a welcome change for any device and a gift that will be pleasantly unexpected.

YOU WILL NEED

30 x 84 cm (12 x 33 in) of base fabric
   for the appliqué

30 x 84 cm (12 x 33 in) of cotton low loft
   quilting wadding (batting)

30 x 84 cm (12 x 33 in) of calico (cotton muslin)
   for the lining

Sewing thread and needle

Various colours of remnant fabric for appliqué

Fabric marker or pencil

Scissors

Appliqué pins

Thread to match appliqué pieces

235 cm (92½ in) of 3 cm (1¼ in) wide cotton
   fabric bias strip

Sewing machine and thread to match bias strip

Pins

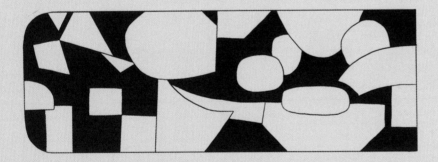

— If you are making your own edging trim, try to cut it on the bias as you will be sewing it around curves. Join shorter pieces as necessary.
— Appliqué pins are shorter than ordinary pins for small shapes, but you can use any pins you have.

— This design can be easily adjusted to make it smaller or larger depending on the size of your device. Another option is to add pockets on the outside to hold accessories like the charger or small things like pens and a notebook.

(1) Place the lining fabric right side down, add the wadding on top, then add the base fabric for the appliqué right side up. (1a) Sew the layers together with a tacking (basting) stitch (see page 17) to keep them together.

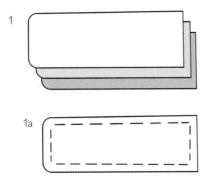

You can use your own shapes for this project or use the templates. When you create your template make sure it includes a 0.5 cm (¼ in) seam allowance all around, and cut out.

(2) Lay out your remnant fabric and decide which colours you want to use for each shape. Place the paper templates on top of the fabric and trace onto the fabric. Cut out with scissors and then position the shapes onto the base cloth. Pin or tack in place to hold the shapes down while you hand sew.

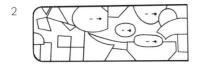

Sew the shapes down, one by one, with the appliqué stitching (see page 17) going through all layers all the way to the back. Thread your needle with a matching colour thread and tie a quilter's knot (see page 15) at one end. Begin sewing by folding under the edge of the fabric shapes by 0.5 cm (¼ in) and holding down the edge with your finger nail. Push the needle from underneath through the folded edge of the appliqué fabric, near the edge. Then go over the fold and down into the base cloth, batting and lining. Move your needle about 1.25 cm (½ in) from the previous stitch and repeat until you go all around the shape. The finished stitching will appear to be perpendicular to the fabric edge. Fasten off with a knot on the reverse. Repeat until all your pieces are sewn down.

Cut a 30 cm (12 in) length of the bias strip. (3) Place this along the short, square end of the appliquéd panel, with right sides together and with edges aligned. With a sewing machine sew in place with a 1 cm (⅜ in) seam allowance. Fold the strip over to the lining side of the panel and fold under the edge. Use a blind stitch (see page 12) to sew down the folded edge.

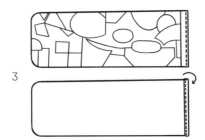

(4) With the appliqué panel laying right side down, fold the edge with the binding over on top to create a pocket 33 cm (13 in) deep with the appliqué on the outside and the lining on the inside. Use the sewing machine to sew the folded edges together at the 2 corners for about 2.5 cm (1 in), to keep the fold in place while you sew the outer binding.

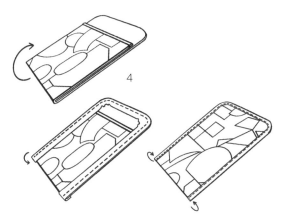

4

Place the remaining bias strip right sides together on the appliqué panel, with edges aligned, starting about 2.5 cm (1 in) beyond one of the bottom corners with the fold. Fold the extended length of the binding over on top of itself to hide the raw end and pin in place. Continue binding along the complete edge until you get back to the first corner, leaving an extra 2.5 cm (1 in) of binding. Sew along the entire edge with a 1 cm (⅜ in) seam allowance. At the last corner, fold the end of the binding over on top of itself to hide the raw edge, as before, and finish sewing the seam allowance. Turn the bias to the other side and fold it under and finish using a blind stitch (see page 12).

Patchwork Stockings

For many, having stockings as part of your holiday celebration is a definite must.
Especially since all those little extra treats and gifts are sometimes the most fun of
all. And of course, there is a long tradition in making your own stocking, as large as
possible. These stockings continue in that tradition and are not only eco-friendly
– since they use up your old sweater scraps – but, with their geometric patchwork,
will also give any mantle a really modern touch.

YOU WILL NEED

Templates on page 154

Sticky tape

3 to 4 old sweaters in neutral tones

Scissors

Sewing machine and thread to coordinate
with the fabrics

Iron

Old pillowcase or pressing cloth

Water-soluble fabric marker

25 cm (¼ yd) of calico (cotton muslin)
for the lining of each stocking

Pins

— When sewing patchwork is to make sure
the seams match up. I find this gives the piece
almost a pattern and feels more structured.
— If you want, you can make patchwork for
the back of the stocking as well.

Copy the templates to the correct size and cut out the shapes. Join up the template pieces, matching the lettered edges, and stick them together with tape to make the complete stocking shape. Cut the sweaters into random pieces if necessary.

This patchwork stocking is made from various remnants of wool and cashmere sweaters. The first thing I do is to group the remnants by colour so that I can choose a cohesive colour palette for each stocking. There is no rule for how to choose colours, but I usually choose 7 or 8 colours with similar tones so the overall feel is a little neutral, some a little light, some a little darker. Or you can simply approach it randomly.

My approach to patching the pieces together tends to be completely intuitive. I start with 2 pieces of relatively small size, differing in shape, and sew them together with a 1 cm (⅜ in) seam allowance. I add a third piece to the long side of the patchwork. I keep rotating and adding. If pieces are too small I join them together before adding to the larger piece. Continue adding pieces until the patchwork covers the template. If you want to patchwork front and back make a second piece.

After you are done sewing, press the piece with an iron. If you want to avoid any scorching of the fibres, place an old pillowcase on top of the piece.

(1) Lay the template onto the patchwork and use the water-soluble marker to trace the outline. Cut around the outline. Use the template to trace and cut the backing piece, either from patchwork or from a single piece of knitted fabric, and 2 pieces of fabric for the lining as well. Remember to reverse the template for the back pieces so you have mirrored pieces.

(2) Place the front and back of the stocking together, edges aligned and with right sides together, and sew around the entire edge, excluding the top, with a 1 cm (⅜ in) seam allowance. Turn right side out.

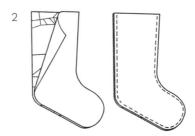

(3) Cut a small strip of sweater about 1.25 cm (½ in) wide and 12.5 cm (5 in) in length leaving the edges raw. Fold it in half and sew to the outside of the stocking with the loop pointing down and the ends on either side of the side seam, so that one end is sewn to the back and one to the front. This will be a loop to hang the stocking.

(4) Place the 2 pieces of lining right sides together and sew along the outside edge with a 1 cm (⅜ in) seam allowance, similar to the outside of the stocking, except leave an opening about 10 cm (4 in) wide along the side so that you can turn the stocking right side out. Do not turn the lining right side out.

(5) Place the outside piece inside the lining (so they will now be right sides together) and sew around the top edge with a 1 cm (⅜ in) seam allowance. Pull the whole

stocking right sides out completely through the unsewn opening in the lining. Stitch the opening in the lining closed.

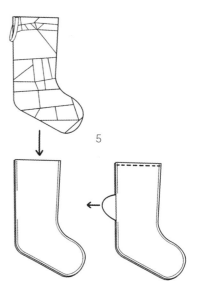

(6) Push the lining inside the stocking. I chose to not do any top stitching along the top with my sewing machine, but you could hand sew a running stitch (see page 16) around the top with a thicker thread to give the top edge a little detail.

Mobile

When thinking of gifts, it's easy to think about utility – after all, we need useful things. But some things have a different purpose; they are objects that adorn your home just because they are interesting and beautiful. A mobile is a sculptural work of art that is so different from the other things that surround us. It hangs, occupying a place that is less easy to define – perhaps near a window, casting shadows on a wall, or moving, providing different shapes and glimpses of colour. This one is made with natural materials and brings warmth with a variety of subtle colours.

YOU WILL NEED

Various pieces of wood veneer

Scrap pieces of plywood

Plastic wrap

Water-based wood glue

Brush or small piece of card to spread glue

2 to 4 clamps

Pencil

Sturdy scissors or kitchen shears

180 grit and fine sandpaper

Wood oil such as linseed or beeswax
   mixed with oil

Soft cloth

Ruler

Drill with approx. 2 mm ($^1/_{16}$-in) drill bit

114 cm (45 in) of waxed cotton thread,
   plain or coloured

46 cm (18 in) and 38 cm (15 in) of 2.28 mm
   ($^3/_{32}$ in) brass wire

Needle nose and round nose pliers

Wire cutters

String to hang mobile

Nail or screw to hang from

—The fastest way to cut veneer is with a sturdy pair of scissors, taking care not to split the veneer too much – although if that does happen that's OK.
— On the 46 cm (18 in) piece of wire make a small loop 14 cm (5.5 in) from one end. On the 38 cm (15 in) wire make a similar loop 13 cm (5 in) from one end. Then make small hooks on all four ends to hang the wood pieces.
— As an option, you can use pieces of thin millboard for the central core between two veneer outer pieces.
— The brass wire should be similar in thickness to a coat hanger.

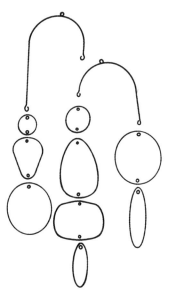

Referring to the above guide, collect pieces of wood veneer in various types and colours, in sizes ranging from 5 x 5 cm (2 x 2 in) to 10 x 15 cm (4 x 6 in). For each individual shape on the template you will need 3 pieces large enough to cover the shape, to make 9 ornaments in total. Arrange the 3 pieces of veneer for each ornament into 2 outside pieces and 1 centre piece. At this point they can remain as squares or rectangles. Arrange each group so that the grain of the outer 2 pieces runs in one direction, while the centre piece runs in a perpendicular direction. This will ensure that each ornament, when glued, remains stronger than veneer layers with grain running in a single direction.

Place a piece of plywood on your table, a little larger than the veneer you are going to glue, and cover with a piece of plastic wrap. On top, place one of the outside pieces of veneer. On top of that, place the central piece of veneer with wood glue spread on both sides. Remember to place it down with the grain perpendicular to the first. Then place the last piece on top, with the grain running the same way as the first piece. Finish the pile with another piece of plastic wrap. Place another piece of plywood on top and clamp tightly. You can also glue and clamp several sets of veneer at the same time, if they are roughly the same size, by repeating this step for each set, making sure to keep each group separated with plastic wrap. Then place plywood down on top of the stack and clamp tightly. Make sure to finish clamping each set before the glue begins to dry. Leave clamped to dry for 24 hours.

After the glue has dried, unclamp and separate each layered piece. Using the template provided, or making your own design, copy the shape of each ornament onto the layered veneers. If you want you can orient the shapes so that they all share a similar grain orientation, or keep it random. Cut each shape out using sturdy scissors or a pair of kitchen shears. Sand the sides smooth to achieve the desired shape with 180 grit sandpaper, and then finish the edges and fronts with a fine grit sandpaper. To bring out the colour of each piece, rub each with a small amount of a wood finish such as linseed oil or beeswax mixed with oil. After a few hours you can wipe dry with a soft cloth.

Working on a table, arrange the ornaments as they would hang in vertical rows of different lengths. I made one with 2 pieces, one with 3, and one with 4. When you have the arrangement you want, mark a spot for holes on the top and bottom of each piece, centred and about 0.5 cm (¼ in) from the outside edge. On the bottom ornament in the row only mark a hole on the top, leaving the bottom edge without one. Drill holes using a small drill bit, about 2 mm (¹⁄₁₆ in). Using 10 cm (4 in) or 12.5 cm (5 in) lengths of waxed thread, tie each ornament in a row together so that they remain about 0.5 cm (¼ in) apart. Knot to secure and then clip or wind and press any tail into the knot. On the topmost ornaments tie a small loop in the thread large enough for the wire.

Clay Resist and Indigo Dyed Pillow

I am a big fan of indigo; I love how the blue catches your eye and you can adjust the strength of the colour with multiple dippings. Creating a resist for your fabric is a nice way to combine imagery with the indigo as a backdrop. It may seem complicated but it's quite easy – you just paint your image and then dip it in the indigo. It's perfect for creating fabric for sewing projects and, because you'll be making a vat of dye, it's possible to make several pieces at the same time. This project goes even further by incorporating embroidery onto the dyed fabric. The pillow front is also quilted providing depth and texture, while the stitching enhances the dyed image with an additional level of detail.

YOU WILL NEED

Template on the front endpapers

Paper and pencil

Tape

53.5 x 53.5 cm (21 x 21 in) of cotton/linen blend fabric for pillow front

53.5 x 53.5 cm (21 x 21 in) of fabric for the pillow back

Water-soluble fabric marker

Clay resist kit

Mixing cup and spatula

Drop cloth to protect work surface

No. 10 round paint brush

Extra strip of cotton/linen blend fabric for dye testing

Indigo dye kit

20 litre (5 gallon) bucket for indigo mixture

Plastic tarp

Rubber gloves

Drying rack

Basin of water

Small amount of gentle fabric soap

53.5 x 53.5 cm (21 x 21 in) of cotton wadding (batting) with a low loft

53.5 x 53.5 cm (21 x 21 in) of calico (cotton muslin) fabric for the reverse of the quilting

Safety pins

Wonderfil spaghetti thread colour SP37

No. 9 embroidery needle

40 cm (16 in) plastic zipper

Sewing machine and matching thread

51 cm (20 in) pillow insert

TIPS

— You can use the same fabric for the pillow back, or a different plain fabric.

— You can simply buy a clay resist kit to use here. I used a clay resist kit from The Love of Colour.

— The clay resist may come through the cloth, so it's good to work on a drop cloth or paper. All the areas that you paint on the cloth will resist the indigo dye when dry. If you make a mistake while painting, the clay resist mixture can be washed out, but be careful not to moisten adjacent areas.

— The clay resist will cause the fabric to pucker as it dries, so tape the pillow front down carefully.

Use the template provided or create your own drawing. If you are using the template, copy it and tape the pieces together if necessary. Place it under the fabric (pillow front), making sure to centre the design. Tape down the drawing and the fabric – the black lines should be visible under the fabric. If not, tape the drawing and fabric on a light source such as a window instead. Trace all the outlines using a water-soluble marker. Keep in mind that the template also shows the stitched lines, but you only need to outline areas that will be painted with the clay resist.

Follow the instructions in the clay resist kit to make the mixture. The mixture can stay in an open container while you work, but it will take you a few days to paint on the clay resist so it's best to keep it stored in an airtight container overnight. Remember to stir the mixture periodically while working to keep the clay from settling to the bottom.

Before you start painting protect your work surface with the drop cloth. Tape down the fabric to prevent it from moving too much as it dries. I started painting from left to right because I am right-handed and worked to the right-hand side. I painted on 2–3 coats in each area, letting each coat dry for a few minutes. If you want a strong resist, then it's a good idea to do several coats because some of the clay resist will start washing out if you make many dips in the indigo. Before you dye the fabric you should do a dye test, so also paint a stripe on the spare strip of fabric using the clay resist. Give it 2–3 coats. Once you finish painting, let all the fabric pieces dry overnight.

119

The indigo dye bath needs to sit overnight before it is used, so follow the instructions in the kit to make it now. I like to use a large bucket so the fabric can move around freely. It's best to sit the bucket on a plastic tarp to make sure any splashes made when dyeing do not stain surrounding areas. Once you have created the mixture, let it sit overnight in a warm place. The indigo mixture should have a greenish hue when it is ready.

Before dyeing make sure you remove any foam or debris from the top of the bucket. The indigo tends to stain so wear rubber gloves and clothes you don't mind getting dye on. First, dip the whole test strip into the bucket, pull it out and let it turn blue. Dip it again but this time do not dip it completely. Repeat about 4–5 times, each time dipping a little less than the previous time – this will give you a gradation of blues from light to dark. Once the final dip turns blue, rinse out the clay resist. The test strip will help determine how many dips you want compared to the white of the areas that had resist. The darker the blue, the more dips you need make. But keep in mind that every time you dip the clay resist will wash off a bit, which may result in the resist area turning from a white to a pale blue. Decide how many dips you want to do.

Now submerge the dry painted cushion front slowly in the bucket, holding the 2 top corners and keeping it submerged for a few minutes. Slowly pull it out of the bucket

and place on a drying rack; you will see the colour go from green to blue. Once it turns blue you can dip it again right away with the fabric still wet. Dip as many times as you need to get the colour you want. Keep in mind that wet fabric looks darker and will appear lighter when dry. I dipped my fabric 3 times.

Once the dyeing is done, place the fabric in a basin of water with a small amount of gentle fabric soap and start moving the fabric around to give it a good rinse. Some of the indigo may rinse off, but this is normal. You will also be washing the clay resist off, revealing the white imagery. When clean, hang the fabric to dry. If you are using the same fabric for the back of the cushion and want it to be the same blue you can repeat the steps to dye this.

The next step is to add stitching detail to the design. Place the wadding on top of the calico quilt backing and the indigo dyed piece right side up on top of the wadding, and join all 3 layers together with a few safety pins. I added running stitches to the design by outlining the shapes and adding more stitches in certain areas to give the design more detail.

(1) Zigzag stitch around the perimeter of the quilted piece and the back piece of the pillow. Place the front and back of the pillow cover right sides together. Along the bottom edge measure where the zipper will go and then

stitch the layers together at the 2 ends (2a) leaving an open unsewn space for the zipper. Open out the pieces and iron the seams flat, including the space for the zipper (2b). Place the zipper underneath, centred in the unsewn space and right side up. Using a zipper foot, sew the zipper in place along both sides and ends.

(3) Fold the pieces right sides facing again and (4) sew around the perimeter of the remaining 3 sides using a 1 cm (⅜ in) seam allowance. (5) Turn the pillow right side out making sure to push out the corners. Place the pillow insert inside and close the zipper.

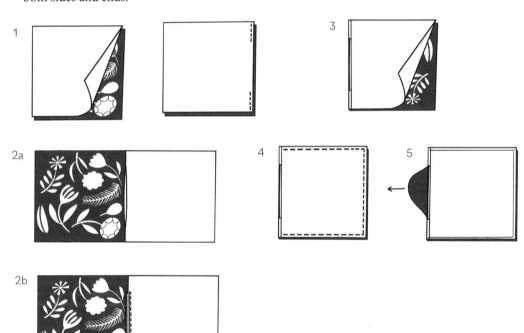

Handbound Books

For some people, notebooks and sketchbooks are the kind of things they have a personal connection with, which is why handmade books are such great gifts for artists and writers, gardeners or old school amateur detectives. In fact, anyone who still understands the utility and beauty of paper and pen, or pencil, to make daily notations or artworks. And a handmade book is so much fun to make – they can be made with so many variations, with many ways to structure and decorate them. For this project I created handbound books in two different varieties: a leather-bound book and a concertina sketch book.

LEATHER-BOUND BOOK

This book has a leather cover that is hand painted, and features a removable notebook insert that can be replaced when the book is filled.

YOU WILL NEED

16.5 x 21 cm (6½ x 8¼ in) of 85–113 g (3–4 oz) vegetable tanned leather

Acrylic leather paint

Paintbrushes

Awl or nail

Leather hole punch to fit elastic cord diameter

Mat to punch on

Corner leather punch (optional)

56 cm (22 in) of 3 mm (⅛ in) elastic cord

9 x 14 cm (3½ x 5½ in) Cahier Moleskine pocket journal or similar

— The cover is sized to fit a Cahier Moleskine pocket journal measuring 9 x 14 cm (3½ x 5½ in). If you want to carry a different size notebook, just extend the distance between the holes on the template and work with a larger piece of leather.
— I used a natural vegetable tanned leather for the book cover, which will darken with age and would be quite lovely just as it is. However,

I wanted to add decoration to the cover so I painted some motifs using Angelus leather paint, which is acrylic based and permanent.
— As a leather alternative you can use Kraftex, which is a durable washable paper – if so you might want to add an additional 4 cm (1½ in) on both short ends so that you can make a more durable folded edge, with the finished size remaining 16.5 x 21 cm (6½ x 8¼ in).

If you want to decorate the cover, paint some motifs of your choice using a leather paint that is acrylic based and permanent. You could also paint the recipient's name or initials in a lovely script on the cover. Let it dry for 10-15 minutes – if you're making several you can paint them all at once to save time.

Mark out the position of your holes. Place the cover right side up with the template on top. Use an awl or nail to make a small mark where the holes will go and then use the hole punch to make the holes. If you are using Kraftex, paper punch the holes then reinforce with grommets. I used a corner punch to round the 4 corners of the cover – if you prefer you can leave the corners square but I feel the round corners gives a nice, finished look. If you're using the Kraftex paper do not round the corners – instead fold the extra width of the front and back inside by about 4 cm (1½ in) to reinforce the edge of the cover.

(1) Fold the elastic cord in half to find the mid-point. With the cover open and working from the inside, feed the folded loop of the elastic down through the centre hole until there is a loop of about 7.5 cm (3 in) on the outside of the cover. If you have trouble feeding the loop through you can use your awl or nail to push it through, or wiggle the awl around to widen the hole slightly. On the inside, feed one loose end down through the second hole from the bottom and then up through the bottom hole. Repeat with the other loose end through the top 2 holes.

Lastly, tie the 2 loose ends together using a double reef knot. It's okay if the cover buckles a little – once you insert the note book it will flatten out. Trim any extra elastic, leaving about a 2.5 cm (1 in) tail.

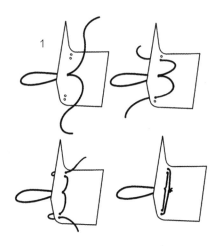

Open the notebook to the centre and slide it underneath the knotted elastic on the inside. Wrap the elastic loop on the outside around the book to keep it closed.

CONCERTINA ACCORDION BOOK

The second handbound book has a hard cover with an interior made from one large sheet of paper that folds neatly in between the covers like an accordion.

WHAT YOU NEED

57 x 75 cm (22½ x 30 in) sheet of drawing or watercolour paper

Ruler and pencil (optional)

Folding bone

Craft knife or scissors

2 pieces of millboard each 14 x 20 cm (5½ x 8 in)

Neutral ph glue

7.5 cm (3 in) wide flat brush

2 pieces of fabric each 17.75 x 24 cm (7 x 9½ in) to cover the millboard

Place the drawing or watercolour paper with the long edges at the top and bottom. Fold twice horizontally to divide it into 3 equal strips with each fold about 19 cm (7½ in) apart. Use a folding bone to score the paper first to make it easier to fold. Unfold it and lay it flat again. Then fold vertically 5 times to divide it into 6 equal strips with each fold about 12.5 (5 in) apart. If you prefer, you can divide the paper up with a ruler first, making small marks with a pencil where you must fold. If your paper is sized differently, adjust the size of your folds accordingly.

Lay the folded paper flat on your table again. You will have 3 horizontal rows separated by 2 horizontal folds. Each row has 6 sections. Use a craft knife or scissors to make a horizontal cut along each of the 2 horizontal folds, the first starting on the right-hand

TIPS

— I used fabric to cover the millboard, but you could also use a decorative paper.

125

edge and finishing at the last vertical fold on the left, the second starting on the left-hand edge and finishing at the last vertical fold on the right (see illustration).

(1) Fold the paper to form the inside pages of the book. With the paper in the same landscape orientation, start folding the first/bottom horizontal row at the loose end by creating an accordion fold, going under and over, until you reach the other side where it is joined to the middle row above. (2) Then, with the first row all folded, fold it underneath the first section of the second/middle row. (3) Fold the second row in the same accordion fold as the first (4). When you reach the last fold, where it is joined to the third row above, fold the entire stack underneath the first section of the third/top row (5). Then, finish folding across the last row in the same manner until all sections are folded. You will end up with a stack of pages with a continuous accordion fold.

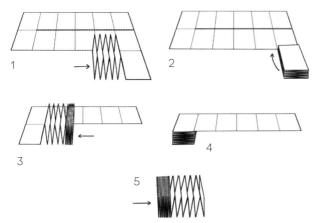

To create the covers for the book, first cover the millboard with the fabric. Start by spreading glue evenly over one side of the millboard with your brush, making sure there are no lumps or areas with more glue that might seep through the fabric. Let it sit for 5–10 seconds. Place the millboard, glue side down, on the centre of the wrong side of the fabric. Flip it over and lightly press the fabric down.

(6) With the cover right side down, cut all 4 corners of the fabric at 45 degrees about 0.25cm (⅛ in) away from the corner of the millboard. Working on one side at a time, apply glue to the edge and the back of the millboard as far as the fabric will wrap around onto the back – about 1 cm (⅜ in). Pull the fabric tightly, fold it over onto the glue and press flat. Repeat on all 4 sides, making sure that the glue is spread evenly and tacky when you are about to stick the fabric down. Repeat steps 4 and 5 with the second piece of millboard and fabric.

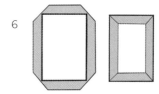

(7) The final step is to glue the covers to the pages. Apply a generous amount of glue to the inside cover, making sure to stay about 0.5 cm (¼ in) away from all 4 edges. With the pages still folded together, place one side of the stack on the glued back side of the cover, making sure to centre the pages on the cover. Repeat on the other side of the book to add the other cover. Place the book underneath something heavy, such as a pile of books, for a few days so that it dries completely and stays flat. When you gift the book you can tie ribbon around it or gift with some nice art pens.

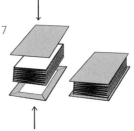

Tool/Gadget Holder

Finding a gift for a craftsperson or maker can be difficult. But one sure way to impress the creative in your life is with something not only useful, but that helps with the important things in life – tools! Especially ones they like to keep with them. I rarely leave my studio without some sort of work to do when I have a free moment, so having a holder for all those little things that easily fits in a bag or pocket is absolutely necessary. Even non-makers may need a little organization with life's everyday items and this holder is quite versatile; it can be made larger or smaller and is easily modified with different compartments.

YOU WILL NEED

75 x 51 cm (30 x 20 in) of waxed canvas

Hera marker

Tape measure or ruler

Scissors

38 x 40.75 cm (15 x 16 in) of calico
  (cotton muslin) for lining

Pencil

17.75 cm (7 in) metal zipper

Sewing machine and matching thread

15 x 0.5 cm (6 x ¼ in) leather pull

Sewing clips

Hole punch

Small grommet

Hammer

101.5 cm (40 in) of 2 mm (¹⁄₁₆ in)
  dark brown leather cord

TIPS

— I chose waxed canvas because of its durability, but any sort of sturdy fabric will do.
— I like using the cord as a closer on the tool holder because it's easier to adjust for different situations depending on what you are carrying. If you would rather, you can also add snaps or a button closure.

Use the marker to mark the waxed canvas and a pencil on the calico, and then cut all your fabric pieces for the tool/gadget roll. From the waxed canvas: two 2.5 x 3 cm (1 x 1¼ in) pieces for the zipper tabs, a 14 x 21.5 cm (5½ x 8½ in) piece for the zipper bottom pocket, a 21.5 x 4 cm (8½ x 1½ in) piece for the zipper top band, a 21.5 x 17.75 cm (8½ x 7 in) piece for the pocket back, a 21.5 x 15 cm (8½ x 6 in) piece for the pocket front and a 26.75 x 51 cm (10.5 x 20in) piece for the body of the holder. From the calico lining: a 14 x 21.5 cm (5½ x 8½ in) piece for the zipper bottom pocket, a 21.5 x 4 cm (8½ x 1½ in) piece for the zipper top band, and a 21.5 x 17.75 cm (8½ x 7 in) piece for the back lining of the zipper pocket.

(1) Start by sewing together the zipper pocket. On each of the 2 zipper tabs make a 0.5 cm (¼ in) fold along one of the long sides. Sew a tab onto either end of the zipper with the fold facing down. Make sure to sew close to the folded edge of the fabric.

(2) To make the zipper pocket, place the zipper right side up on top of the lining zipper bottom pocket, aligned along the edge of the long side. Place the waxed canvas zipper bottom pocket right side down on top of the zipper, also aligned along the edge of the long side and making sure all 3 layers are centred on the zipper. Sew the layers together along the long side using a 1 cm (⅜ in) seam allowance. Fold the lining and the wax canvas away from the zipper so that the right sides are facing out. At this point you can sew an optional top stitch just below the zipper (on mine I chose to not sew a top stitch).

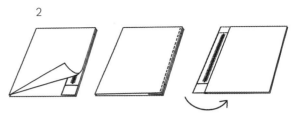

(3) Now place the waxed canvas zipper top band right side down on top of the other side of the zipper, centred and aligned along the long edge. Sew the 2 layers together using a 1 cm (⅜ in) seam allowance. Fold the band over away from the zipper so the right side is facing out and top stitch along the edge, close to the zipper to keep the top section flat.

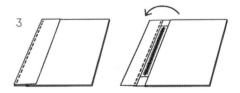

(4) Place the lining for the back of the zipper pocket right side down on top of the right side of the whole zipper panel, centred and aligned along the top edge. Sew along the top edge using a 1 cm (⅜ in) seam allowance. Turn the lining over to the back, make a nice fold along the seam, and sew a top stitch along the edge of the waxed canvas. Add the leather pull to the pull of the zipper.

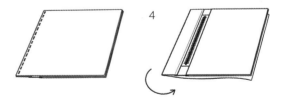

(5) Now make the double pocket. On one long side of the waxed canvas back pocket and front pocket pieces, turn the fabric under by 0.5 cm (¼ in) twice and sew down along the edge of the first fold. Fold the shorter piece in half along the long side to

make a centre line crease. Place the smaller piece right side up on top of the larger piece, also right side up, with all 3 unsewn edges aligned. Stitch along the centre crease to create a double pocket.

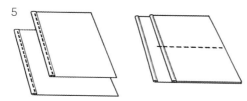

5

(6) Lay the body piece of the tool holder flat, with the interior side facing up. Place the zipper pocket and double pocket on top facing up. The zipper pocket should be placed on one end so that its unsewn bottom edge is about 2 cm (¾ in) from one short end of the body and centred from side to side. Place the double pocket about 4 cm (1½ in) away from the top of the zipper pocket, also centred. Fasten both temporarily in place with some sewing clips. At the bottom of the double pocket turn the 2 layers of fabric under by about 0.5 cm (¼ in) and stitch close to the folded edge. Sew a second line by guiding the edge of the sewing foot along the first stitched line.

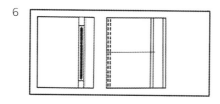

6

(7) Sew a rolled hem all around the perimeter of the tool/gadget holder by folding over the waxed canvas by 0.5 cm (¼ in) twice, making sure that the second fold goes over all unsewn edges of the pockets. Sew along the inside edge of the

rolled hem as close as you can. As you approach a corner make sure to turn the next side under to create a neat corner.

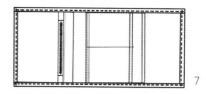

7

(8) Fold the zipper pocket over so the outer edge of the body is aligned with the top of the double pocket. The remaining portion will then fold down and serve as a flap.

Measure a point in the centre of the flap and about 2 cm (¾ in) from its edge. Using a hole punch, create a small hole for a grommet, then hammer the grommet into the hole. Tie a knot very close to one end of the leather cord and feed it through the hole from the inside. Tie another knot on the outside of the hole to secure the cord in place. Wrap the cord around the entire folded tool holder and tuck the loose end into the wrap.

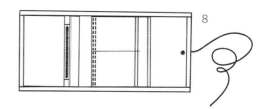

8

Eco-Printed Silk Scarf

There has been a huge surge in popularity for natural and ecological ways to print and dye fabric. And when you think about it, it's such an incredible idea to have access to everything you need to make the most beautiful items from our gardens, or from the kitchen. In fact we are surrounded by materials that can add amazing colours and surface qualities to even the simplest of textile projects. This project showcases the beautiful patterns you can make from flowers and plants. And an item such as a scarf is particularly well suited to highlight the random shapes, colours and unique textures that can be achieved from eco-printing.

YOU WILL NEED

91.5 x 91.5 cm (36 x 36 in) pre-made
  plain silk scarf

Scales

Alum acetate for mordanting

Large pot to boil water

Small amount of detergent

Large bucket or basin for the mordant

Pot with lid and matching strainer to steam

Dried flowers, plant matter and cochineal

String to wrap bundle

Drying rack

Iron

TIPS

— Use dried flowers or plant matter such as such as calendula, marigold, chamomile, coreopsis, hopi sunflower seeds or onion skins.
— The mordant is a necessary first step in natural dying to help the dye bond with the fibres thus improving lightfastness and washability. There are many other mordants that you can use, such as more traditional tannins, but I like how aluminium acetate gives you bright colours and won't change the colour of the base

fabric – which is especially useful when you are trying to capture the bright and fresh colours of flowers.
— Typically, with many colours, the more alum you use the deeper the colour.
— Remember that all pots and utensils that you use for natural dyeing should not be used for preparing food. You can get inexpensive pots from the charity shop or use an old pot.

You will need to use 10–20 per cent of alum acetate to the weight of fabric. So, for example, if your fabric weighs 100 g (3½ oz) you will use about 20 g (¾ oz) of alum. Once you have calculated your percentage, wash the scarf by adding a bit of detergent to a pot of water, bringing to a boil and simmering the fabric for about 20 mins. Let cool and rinse the fabric. Then fill a container large enough for the fabric you're using with hot water – this process will not need a heat source so you can use a bucket or large basin. Add the alum acetate and mix thoroughly. Place the washed fabric in the container for about 45 minutes making sure to occasionally stir so the fabric gets an overall soak. Once you are done there is no need to rinse the fabric again. While the scarf is soaking, start heating up a few centimetres/inches of water in the metal pot with the strainer so that it will be ready when you finish the next step.

Making sure the fabric is wet, lay it on a table on an angle (so that it looks like a diamond shape), completely spread out and flat. Randomly sprinkle the flowers and plants on the lower half of the diamond shape, keeping the upper half empty. When you are finished, fold the upper half of the fabric down onto the lower half with the plant matter. It will now look like an inverted triangle. Make sure that there is even coverage of plant matter right up to the fold so that you don't end up with a gap.

Roll the scarf up, starting with the bottom corner and rolling the fabric in a fairly tight manner right to the top. You can also start on the long side but I find it a bit harder to control. Once it is all rolled up, start at one end and coil the entire roll into a flat but tight circle. Wrap the string around the circle and bundle it up tightly. Make sure to finish with a knot so that it does not loosen while steaming. Place the strainer over the pot. When the water is boiling, place the bundle on the strainer so that the fabric doesn't touch the water and cover the pot with a lid. Let it steam inside the pot for one hour, adding more water if necessary. When ready, remove the scarf and run it under cold water before unbundling. If you are making more than one scarf you can steam them all at once to save time.

Cut off the string and start to unbundle, shaking off any used plant matter. Give the scarf a little rinse to remove any smaller bits. Hang to dry and press with a hot iron to get out any wrinkles. Because you mordanted the fabric beforehand, the item can be washed and will be colour fast. To keep the colours vibrant, wash by hand and keep out of direct sunlight.

Basket Bag

Most people have no shortage of bags including everyday totes for running around, which makes it challenging when giving one as a gift. Which is why making a bag, especially one that is as versatile as it is lovely, makes so much sense. This bag takes its cue from a basket – it's perfect for a casual day of shopping, its wide soft strap is comfortable on your arm, and it can be made with your most stylish fabric. And if you'd rather, it's equally useful at home as a small storage bin! I made two sizes, both of which I thought would be useful. But it can be made in any size with any fabric or colour.

YOU WILL NEED

2 pieces of fabric each 46 x 42.5 cm
  (18 x 16¾ in) for the large bag

16.5 x 33 cm (6½ x 13 in) of fabric
  for the large bag strap/handle

2 pieces of canvas lining each 46 x 42.5 cm
(18 x 16¾ in) for the large bag lining

2 pieces of fabric each 39.5 x 30 cm
  (15½ x 12 in) for the small bag

15 x 30 cm (6 x 12 in) of fabric for
  the small bag strap/handle

2 pieces of canvas lining each 39.5 x 30 cm
  (15½ x 12 in) for the small bag

Ruler

Water-soluble fabric marker or pencil,
  or chalk pencil for dark coloured fabric

Scissors

Fusible (iron-on) interfacing for the handle
  (optional)

Sewing machine and matching thread

Iron

Pins

— For this project I used some of my woven fabric because I like the texture and I find the heavier weight to be suitable for this bag. Any similarly weighted fabric will do, or you can find a blanket, an old coat or even a small woven rug that would also work well for this project.

— I didn't include an interior pocket for this project, but feel free to add one if you wish – sew it to the right side of one of the lining pieces before you sew the lining together.

Start by cutting out the corners on the bag pieces and the lining to make it easier to create the gusset. For the large bag mark and cut out an 11.5 cm (4½ in) square in each bottom corner, and for the small bag mark and cut out a 7.5 cm (3 in) square in each bottom corner. Zigzag stitch around the outer fabric if you are using something that frays easily or use an overlocker (serger) if you have one. If using, cut the interfacing to match the handle pieces.

(1) Place the outer 2 fabric pieces right sides facing with edges aligned and sew the sides and bottom using a 1 cm (⅜ in) seam allowance, leaving the top opening and gusset unsewn. For the gussets fold the raw edges together so that they become one single straight seam, with the seams of the side and bottom aligned. Sew them together using a 1 cm (⅜ in) seam allowance. Turn the fabric right sides out. Repeat to sew the lining except leave a 10 cm (4 in) opening midway along one side. Leave right sides facing in.

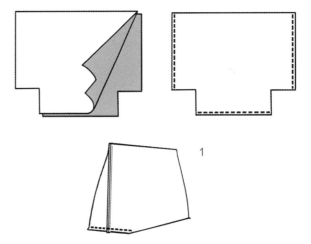

1

(2) Place the interfacing on the wrong side of the handle fabric and iron it on. Fold the fabric in half lengthwise with right sides facing each other. Sew along the edge with a 1 cm (⅜ in) seam allowance leaving the 2 ends unsewn. Turn the handle right sides out and adjust it so that the sewn seam runs along the centre of the handle.

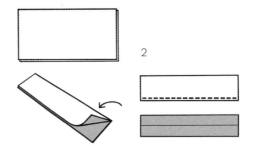

2

Take one end of the handle and place it upside down on the front of the bag, with the seam facing out (and good side facing the bag) so that the short unsewn end is aligned with the top edge of the bag. Pin in place near the top, making sure that it is in the centre of the bag. Take the other end of the handle and pin at the centre on the opposite side of the bag. To do this the handle will travel underneath the bag which will bunch it up (that's ok). Sew the 2 edges of the handle to the bag very close to the edge. This will just tack the handle in place and will not be seen.

(3) Place the outer part of the bag with the handle sewn in place inside the lining with right sides facing each other and the top edges and seams aligned. Sew around the entire top edge of the bag with a 1 cm (⅜ in) seam allowance.

(4) Pull the bag right sides out through the unsewn gap in the lining and then sew the gap closed very close to the edge using a sewing machine, or by hand with a whip stitch (see page 16). Push the lining inside the bag and adjust the handle so that it's sitting at the top of the bag.

(5) The last step is to sew a top stitch with a sewing machine round the top edge of the bag just below the handle. If you want to skip this step you can press with an iron or hand sew a running stitch (see page 16) on the edge instead.

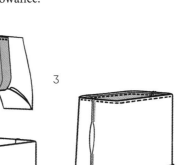

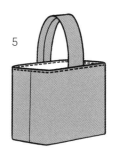

Stencilled Fabric Throw

There are so many uses for a throw; using it to cuddle on a couch, as a picnic blanket or even as wall art. And when it comes to adding surface design, one of the simplest methods that can easily be done at home without any special equipment is printing by stencilling. There is so much potential playing with shapes and patterns and colour. I wanted to make a throw with an unexpected pattern of a simple, randomly placed motifs, which was also subtle enough to blend into any room with a subdued colour palette. Of course, as a gift, this pattern can be easily modified to accommodate different shapes, colours or fabrics to suit the person you have in mind.

YOU WILL NEED

142.25 x 155 cm (56 x 61 in) linen base fabric

Iron

Scissors

Sewing machine and matching thread (optional)

Permanent marker

Template on page 155

Shelf lining paper for the stencil

Cutting mat

Craft knife

Textile ink

Plate or tray for ink

2 cm (¾ in) stencil brush

Old pillowcase for pressing

TIPS

— Any size base fabric will do, just make sure to add 2.5 cm (1 in) in both directions to your desired finished size. My base fabric was 142.25 x 155 cm (56 x 61 in), with a finished size of 139.75 x 152.5 cm (55 x 60 in).
— If you want to create a frayed edge in a tumble dryer, add a few centimetres/inches in both directions when cutting to size before washing to accommodate some shrinkage.
— I used a linen fabric as it is good to print on. You could also use a smooth cotton.

— When stencilling the design, only use an up-and-down movement, never a side-to-side movement because this will cause ink to go under the stencil causing the image to bleed so you won't get a clean edge.
— Washing the fabric first removes any sizing. Sizing is used in fabric to make it stiff, like a starch so washing it out of the fabric makes the ink adhere better.

Wash the fabric before printing so that any sizing is removed and it will take the ink nicely. Press when dry and then cut your fabric to size if necessary. I wanted my throw to have a clean edge so I added a rolled hem on all sides with a sewing machine. A frayed edge could have a nice look as well – create a frayed edge by pulling out the threads or, after you wash the fabric, place it in the dryer and it will naturally fray.

Using a permanent marker, draw your design onto the shelf paper. Make sure the shelf paper is large enough so there is at least 7.5 cm (3 in) or 10 cm (4 in) all around your design. You can draw your design directly or, because the shelf paper and backing is somewhat transparent, it may be possible to trace a drawing placed underneath. Shelf paper has a smooth side on top with a sticky side underneath that is protected by a backing film. Make sure to draw your design on the smooth side, not the backing, and draw so that it is right side up. Keep your design simple, such as a single shape or form, because you will be repositioning this template after each print to make your repeat pattern and fine detail may get damaged along the way.

Place the shelf paper on top of a cutting mat with your drawing on the smooth side facing up, and the backing facing down. Cut around the drawing with the craft knife, removing the inside piece. The stencil you will work with is the outside piece, with your design in the form of an opening. You can also trim the overall size of the shelf paper if you need to, because it only needs to be a square or rectangle about 7.5 cm (3 in) or 10 cm (4 in) larger all around than your design.

Peel the backing paper off your template exposing the sticky side. Place the template,

sticky side down, onto your fabric on an area that you want to print and lightly press down around the opening. Spread a little ink onto the plate or tray and dab your stencil brush, using an up and down motion, into the ink to get an even coat on the brush. Start applying the ink to the fabric along the outside edge of your motif with your brush half on the stencil and half on the fabric and using an up-and-down motion. Work your way to the centre of your motif, moving the brush continuously. Try to keep the inked surface even by adding more ink to the brush as you run out.

When you have finished an area, carefully lift the stencil from one corner (with clean fingers) and reposition it where you want the next print. You can tap the stencil down to stick it to the fabric where there is no ink on the stencil, but you don't really need to worry about the stencil moving and the dabbing movement of the brush will press it down along the edges as you work.

Keep repeating the instructions in step 5 every time you place down the stencil. Try to keep the pattern placement random, occasionally rotating the design so that it appears somewhat different each time. The spacing is up to you but try to avoid placing the stencil on top of inked areas that are not fully dry yet. Keep printing until the entire throw is covered with the motif.

When the ink dries, use an iron with dry heat to heat set the entire fabric so that it can be washed. Press both the front and back for 3–5 minutes, constantly moving your iron. To keep your iron clean, avoid any direct contact with the ink by placing a cloth, such as an old pillowcase, on top of the printed areas as you work. You can also put the fabric in the dryer for 20 minutes on high heat.

Bottle Holder

Holidays are full of gatherings and arriving with a bottle of something is always a thoughtful gesture. This rope bottle holder is easy to make and perfect for carrying any type of bottle, such as wine or water, and – unlike typical wrapping – the holder itself becomes part of the gift, something that can be reused every day while on outings without any added fuss.

YOU WILL NEED

Reusable water bottle for armature

Masking tape

4 strands of rope each 0.5 cm (¼ in) thick and 279.5 cm (110 in) long

1 strand of rope 0.5 cm (¼ in) thick and 152.5 cm (60 in) long for the handle cover

Scissors

TIPS

— If you want to make the bottle holder for a water bottle instead of a wine bottle, you will need the four pieces of rope each to be 228.5 cm (90 in) long.

Start by creating an armature to work on while tying the knots. A reusable water bottle, with the lid removed, taped upside down to your worktable works well. Fold the 4 strands of rope in half to find the mid-point. Then, with all 4 strands aligned and parallel to each other, place them on top of the inverted bottle, with the mid-point centred on the bottle and running in a vertical direction. Place a piece of masking tape just above the mid-point to hold them all in place on the bottle.

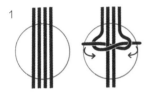

(1) Begin by joining all 4 strands with a starting knot. Only the left and right strands will be used to tie a simple knot around the 2 centre strands, which will remain stationary.

(2) Take the left-hand strand and place it horizontally over the centre strands, and the right-hand strand horizontally under the centre strands. Then feed the left-hand strand through the loop created on the right, and the right-hand strand through the loop on the left. Pull each strand so that the knot created sits at the centre of the bottle. Next, tie the left and right strands together one more time in the same manner, with the left strand coming back over the centre strands and the right strand under, then through the loops. Finish the knot by pulling tight.

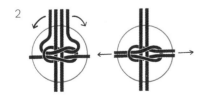

Remove the tape holding the 4 strands of rope at the top and bring down the left and right strand so that you now have a pair of horizontal strands, running left and right, and a pair of vertical strands running up and down, all tied together with the centre knot. Place the tape back where it was so that it now only holds 2 vertical strands.

(3) Next, tie the 2 strands in each pair together with a series of reef knots. Each reef knot consists of 2 simple ties, not unlike when making a bow tie. Start by tying one of the pairs together with the strands going under and over the other. Adjust the knot so that it is located at the edge of the bottle. Repeat this one more time but in reverse so the strands go over then under. This will make a nice symmetrical knot that sits flat. If your knot seems twisted, then undo and try again. Finish the knot by pulling tight. Repeat with the other pairs of rope, taking care to keep the knots all equally spaced, rotating and readjusting the tape as you go. You will end up with 4 knots.

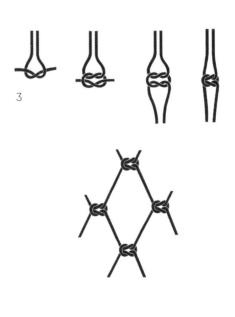

Continue this process, making the same knots to create a lattice around the side of the bottle. However, at this point you will start tying together 2 adjacent strands from different pairs – 1 strand from a pair that ran horizontally with one strand that ran vertically. The lattice you create will now consists of strands on the diagonal. Keep the lengths between knots consistent – I found about 3 cm (1¼ in) to 4 cm (1½ in) worked well. Make one row of knots at a time, working around the bottle, rotating it as necessary, then move on to the next row below. Continue until the entire bottle is covered or the lattice is a desired length.

You will now have 4 knots, each with 2 strands of rope at the unfinished end of the lattice. The first part of the handle will consist of 2 strands from one of the knots hanging stationary, while 1 strand from the knot to the left and 1 strand from the knot to the right are tied around them in the same square knot as the lattice above. Start tying the knots about 3 cm (1¼ in) below the knot above and repeat the knots to create a continuous row about 6.5 cm (2.5 in) to 7.5 cm (3 in) long or about 7 or 8 knots. Make sure all knots are pulled tight. At the end of this section, you will still have 4 strands of rope extending down. Repeat this with the remaining 4 strands of rope on the opposite side.

(4) Remove your work from the water bottle and lay it flat on a table with the 2 handle sections extending toward you. Take the 4 loose strands from each side and overlap them on top of each other where you will make a handle, about 10 cm (4 in) in length. Any extra lengths will be trimmed later. Knot the end of the separate strand of rope for the handle cover. Fold the knotted end over so

that the rope is doubled over for about 20 cm (8 in). Lay this section of the rope along on top of the other 8 strands of the handle so that both the knotted end and the folded loop extend about 5 cm (2 in) beyond the handle area on either side.

4

(5) Holding the 8 strands together with one hand, use the extended loose end of the handle cover rope to bundle them all together. Start wrapping on the side with the knotted end to make a tightly bound coil around the bundle. Continue until your coil is about 9 cm (3½ in) long. To secure the loose end of the handle rope, place it into the folded loop and firmly pull on the knotted end. This will pull the loose end and secure it inside the coil. Then, pull on all the loose ends of the strands on each side of the coiled handle to tighten everything up. Lastly, trim all the loose strands off with scissors close to the coiled handle.

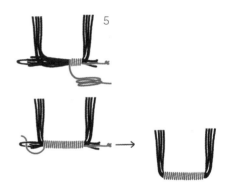

5

Clay Trays with Textured Pattern

Clay and ceramics have a timeless quality. Whether finely crafted or simply shaped by hand where all the marks are left visible, they always speak of that connection between making and utility. And these are definitely useful – a small tray for your hallway or a set on your dresser for all your little things like jewellery or keys. I've decorated these ones with geometric patterns, made from found objects pressed into the wet clay. The clay is self hardening and doesn't require any equipment or technical know-how. You just need your hands.

YOU WILL NEED

500 g (1⅛ lb) pack of air-dry clay

Found objects to push into the clay

Clean sponge (optional)

Piece of plastic sheet large enough
   to loosely cover the tray

Fine sandpaper (grit 220)

Face mask

Damp cloth

Clear matte gel medium

Paint brush

— The technique I used to create these pieces is called pinch pot and I used White Sculpt Dry clay.

— Don't add any water to the clay while forming the bowls; the pinching process itself will soften the clay as you work. If you find that it gets too soft or floppy, let it sit for a few minutes to firm up a bit before continuing.

— The air dry clay is very forgiving and any mistakes or surface marks can easily be mended – use a damp sponge to smooth out any bumps.

To make the smaller trays, take a ball of clay around 4 cm (1½ in) in diameter and stick your thumb into the middle to create an indentation. Start pinching the edges while rotating the clay, slowly working to form a tray shape. The walls will be thick at first but will become thinner and thinner as you work. Keep the walls a similar thickness, with an edge and overall shape that you are happy with.

To create the larger tray, start with a ball of clay about 11.5 cm (4½ in) in diameter. Make the tray in a similar fashion to step 1, pinching around to form an oblong shape and working from the centre to the edge, from thick to thin. Let it sit for a few minutes to firm up if you find that the shape has too much movement. Try to pinch the walls to a thickness of about 0.25cm (⅛ in). You don't want them to be too thin because it will make the tray very fragile and if they are too thick they might crack.

Small found objects, such as hardware or pieces of wood, can be used to create patterns in the wet clay. It's a good idea to test what you have in a small ball of clay first to make sure you like the texture it makes. Hold the tray in the palm of your hand so that the entire underside is supported by the curve of your hand, otherwise you may risk breaking the piece. Gently push the object into the clay – not too far, just a gentle indent. Repeat, trying to be very random with the placemen so the pattern is not too uniform. Once you are done, give the edges a bit of a clean with a finger dipped in water or using a clean sponge.

Set the piece aside to dry out, loosely covered with a piece of plastic so that it does not dry too quickly – this will also prevent any cracking. If some cracking does occur, gently work a little wet clay into the crack and smooth with your fingers. Try also to flip the piece occasionally so that it has even flow of air all around.

After the pieces are completely dry, use a fine sandpaper to smooth out any bumps. Make sure to wear a face mask so you don't breathe in the dust. Give the piece a wipe with a damp cloth to remove any dust and then apply a thin layer of gel medium to the entire surface with a brush. Gel medium comes in a variety or surface qualities and will seal the clay so that it is easy to clean when in use.

RESOURCES

DMC THREADS
www.dmc.com/us/
Cotton floss, Transfer paper, bamboo hoops, fabric, embroidery needles

LEE VALLEY
www.leevalley.com/en-ca
Brass sheet

ANY ART SUPPLY STORE
Sculpey, Kraft paper, coloured drawing paper, glue stick (hot and for paper), acrylic paint, brass wire

CANSON PAPER
INGRES 27 LB/100 GSM #48 CREAM

WOOL, MERINO AND CASHMERE SCRAPS
www.sartoria.ca/products/1-lb-fine-knit-merino-cashmere-scraps

PEBEO
Ceramic paint
https://en.pebeo.com/catalogue/famille/p150-colours/porcelaine

CLAY RESIST KIT AND INDIGO DYE
www.juliesinden.com/collections/natural-dyes

BOTANICAL DYED KITS
www.petalandhank.com/en-ca

FABRIC AND NATURAL DYES
www.maiwa.com/

THREADS
www.wonderfil.ca/

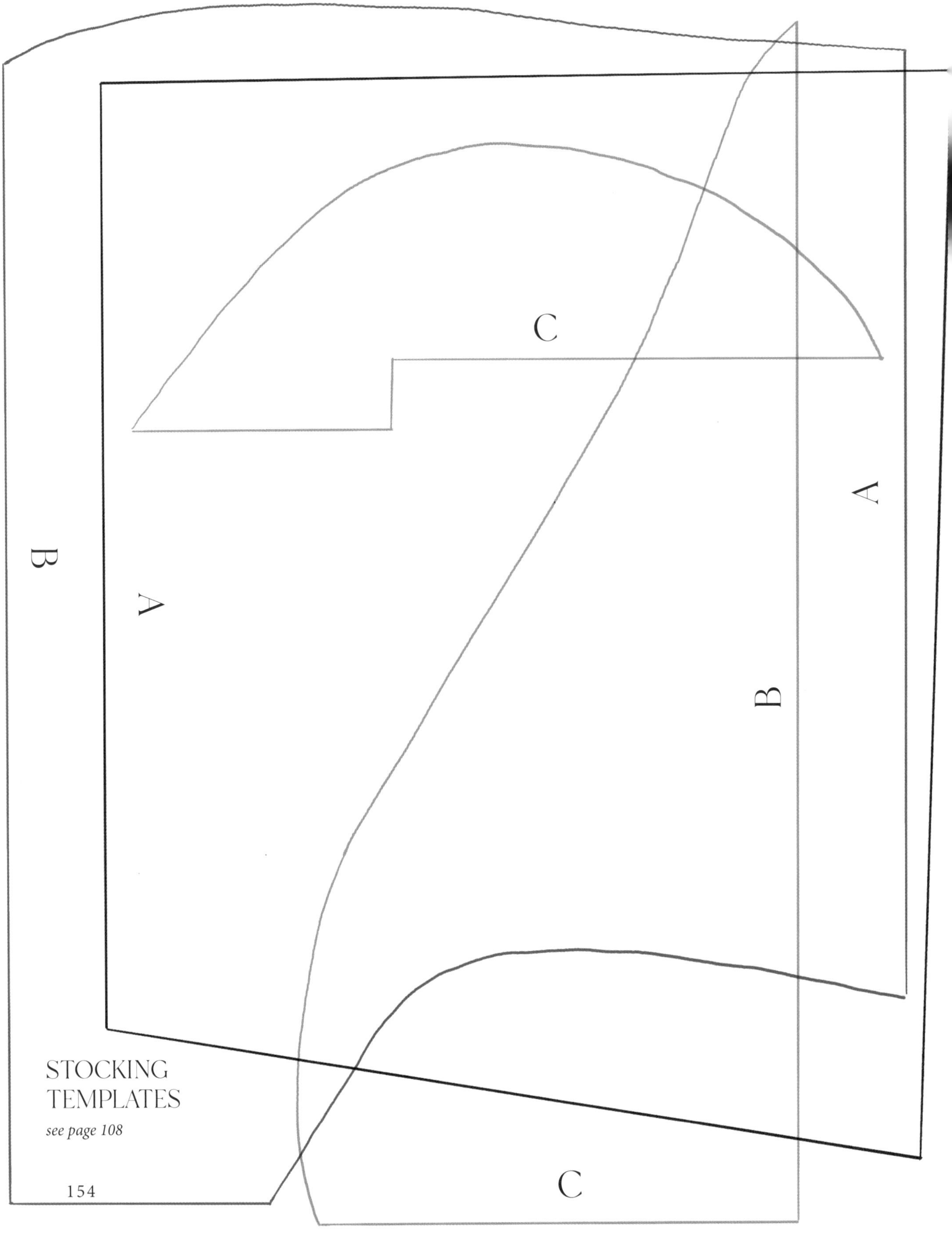

C

A

B

A

B

C

STOCKING
TEMPLATES
see page 108

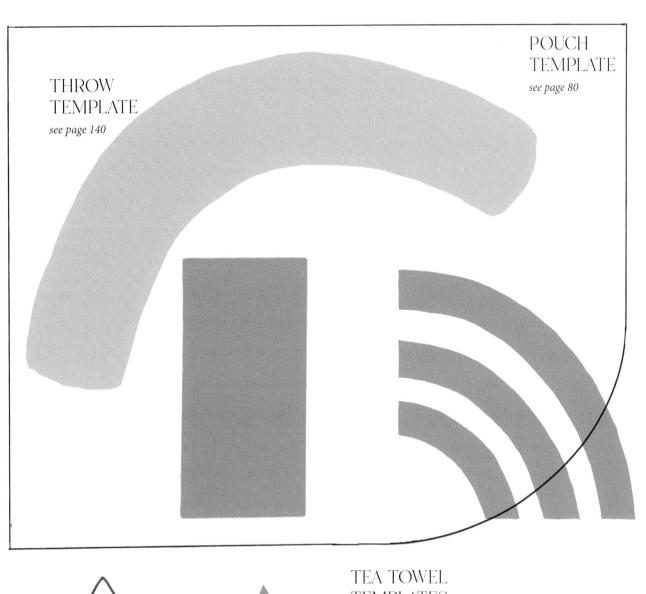

THROW
TEMPLATE
see page 140

POUCH
TEMPLATE
see page 80

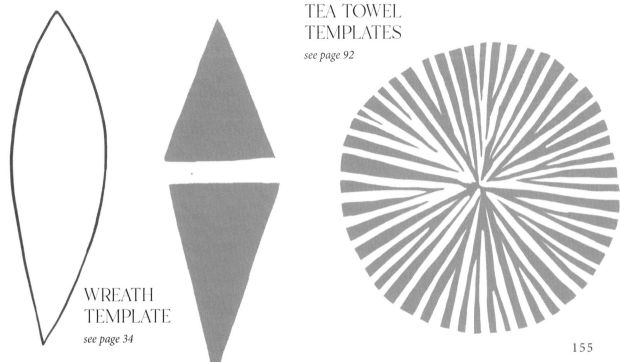

TEA TOWEL
TEMPLATES
see page 92

WREATH
TEMPLATE
see page 34

PAPER
GARLAND
TEMPLATE

see page 30

C

D

B

SIMPLE MITTS
TEMPLATES

see page 88

TABLECOTH
TEMPLATE
see page 38

A

PLACE SETTING
TEMPLATES
see page 20

AUTHOR

Arounna Khounnoraj is an artist and maker living in Canada, where she immigrated with her family from Laos at the age of four. Her education includes a master's degree in fine arts in sculpture and ceramics, but it was through subsequent art residencies that she found her current focus in fibre arts with an emphasis on surface design techniques and textile printing. In 2002, she, along with her husband, John Booth, cofounded **bookhou**, a multidisciplinary studio where Arounna furthered her interest in screen printing and block printing as a means of translating her drawings onto fabric. Her use of hand-drawn imagery and botanical references contributed to a full range of items, such as home goods and personal accessories – including bags. Her use of natural materials, combined with her ever-expanding interest in various forms of stitchwork, such as embroidery and punch needle, gives her work all the qualities of handmade, slow design.

Arounna has collaborated with artists and manufacturers both locally and internationally. She has created two fabric collections with Free Spirit and is currently working on new textile designs for Kokka in Japan. She has also collaborated with Socksappeal and Roots Canada, creating products with her designs.

She has complemented her studio work by teaching workshops on various techniques all over the globe and has expanded this work with a large social media presence, which includes her popular videos on stitching techniques, as well as her studio explorations.

She has done online workshops for the past few years and has created teaching videos with The Crafter's Box and Creativebug. Her videos have helped to popularize a renewed interest in punch-needle techniques. In 2019, she published her first book, *Punch Needle: Master the Art of Punch Needling Accessories for You and Your Home*. In 2020, she released *Visible Mending*, which introduced mending and the reuse of clothing as a personal and hands-on way to address issues of overconsumption and fast fashion in the textile industry. Her third book, *Embroidery*, was released in 2022.

Arounna currently lives in Toronto and Montreal, Canada. Her work can be found at www.bookhou.com and on Instagram @bookhou.

ACKNOWLEDGEMENTS

Thank you to everyone at Quadrille Craft, especially to Harriet Butt and Claire Rochford for being so supportive and for designing a beautiful book. Thank you also to Marie Clayton for editing my words.

Thank you to Laura Edwards for photographing and to Polly Webb-Wilson for her styling work and for modelling some of the projects.

To all the people who support me from near and far; my dear friends, my amazing mum Sengchanh and the Booths, and all of you who follow my process on social media – your positive energy makes my every day brighter.

To my children Lliam and Piper, you two are my heart and I love you both dearly. A big thank you and lots of love to John for your endless support in life and business and for helping me make sense of my words; without you by my side none of this would be possible. xx

Managing Director Sarah Lavelle
Senior Commissioning Editor Harriet Butt
Assistant Editor Oreolu Grillo
Head of Design Claire Rochford
Photographer Laura Edwards
Photographer's Assistant Matthew Hague and Jo Cowan
Props Stylist Polly Webb-Wilson
Production Director Stephen Lang
Production Controller Sabeena Atchia

Published in 2023 by Quadrille, an imprint of Hardie Grant Publishing

Quadrille
52–54 Southwark Street
London SE1 1UN
quadrille.com

text © Arounna Khounnoraj 2023
photography © Laura Edwards 2023
design © Quadrille 2023

Reprinted in 2023
10 9 8 7 6 5 4 3 2

ISBN 978 183 783 066 4

Printed with soy inks in China

FSC
www.fsc.org
MIX
Paper | Supporting responsible forestry
FSC™ C020056